EGYPT

Jack Altman

GW00482041

JPMGUIDES

ancient civilization

CONTENTS

land of the pharaohs

marine splendours

life in the desert

THIS WAY EGYPT

Yes, this is indeed the land of the pharaohs. You can see their pyramids from downtown Cairo. These marvels of Egypt are not way out in the desert. They are there on the doorstep, more than 4,500 years old and still standing proud and strong. The desert comes right to the edge of town. The pyramids are in the suburbs.

Most of Egypt's ancient monuments are part and parcel of the daily scene. All along the edges of the fertile Nile Valley, the dry desert climate has preserved the colossal temples of gods and kings, the brilliant colours of ancient wall-paintings, the fabulous jewels of Tutankhamun. They are not the remote and dusty preserve of remote and dusty scholars, but the glowing, vibrant heritage of a warm-blooded nation.

There are no more friendly, generous people than the Egyptians of today, and their link with that glorious past is unbroken. You may still spot in the noble profile of a merchant selling gold and silver in the bazaar a visible kinship with an ancient prince or courtier depicted in the royal tombs. In the fields of the Nile Valley, you'll see peasants using much the same hoes to till the soil and pumps to water the crops that served their ancestors in pharaonic times.

But the hotel and resort facilities are resolutely modern. Opposite the pyramids of Giza and next door to the temples of Luxor are havens of air-conditioned comfort, dining rooms serving a choice of exotic Middle Eastern fare or a wide variety of European cuisines, and sparkling swimming pools for a cool, refreshing dip.

The Lie of the Land

The Nile river dictates the story of Egypt. The fertility of its valley and the Delta spilling into the Mediterranean have made it the envy of its western neighbours in Libya and its eastern neighbours in Saudi Arabia, Jordan and Israel.

Geographers still wonder that the Nile has not simply dried up as it flows down from the highlands of Ethiopia through Sudan to fight its way across the arid

A glorious sunrise. Egypt's early morning sights reward early risers. For one of the most spectacular sunrises anywhere in the world, even hard-boiled atheists make the pre-dawn pilgrimage from St Catherine's Monastery up **Gebel Musa** (Mount Moses), identified by most Biblical scholars as Mount Sinai. The sight of the craggy landscape changing in colour from blue to purple to crimson and gold is positively hypnotic.

istockphoto.com/Rihak

wilderness of the world's greatest desert, the Sahara. Since 1964, modern technology has given this miracle a hand by harnessing those waters from tropical Africa with the great Aswan Dam. You could squeeze Britain, France and Italy into the country's total area, 1,002,000 sq km (386,900 sq miles), but less than 4 per cent of it is inhabited or farmed. Apart from a dwindling number of Bedouin nomads, a population of 77.5 million lives in the Nile Valley, the Delta, a few oases in the Western Desert, a narrow coastal strip along the Mediterranean and Red Sea, and some villages in the Sinai.

The Nile Valley is a refreshing sight amidst the desert, fields of corn, sugar cane and cotton with an occasional grove of casuarina or date palms for shade. Extending some 24 km (15 miles) at its widest, near Faiyum south of Cairo, the valley is usually around 10 km (6 miles) wide, but can shrink to a hundred metres or so further south. In the deserts east and west of the river, few hills rise above the plain.

The Cities

Cairo is a huge chaotic metropolis, but the good nature of its citizens makes it somehow manageable. Population estimates stopped counting when they reached 18 million. The traffic hurtles along at breakneck speed —when it can escape the jams. Just learn to adopt the relaxed pace of the pedestrians and you'll come to no harm. Shopkeepers, waiters and taxi-drivers here have discovered long ago that cheerfulness is the key to survival. If you do feel like an adventure, try the Metro underground railway. It's a great way of beating the traffic and getting to know the friendly people of Cairo.

The old Egyptian Museum on Tahrir Square is a marvel, and finally undergoing much-needed reorganization, while a grand new modern one is being built near the Pyramids. The capital's mosques are among the finest and most revered in Islam. Indeed, Cairo's cinema, universities and Islamic art and architecture have kept it as undisputed leader of Arab culture. The Khan El Khalili bazaar is one of the world's most colourful markets. In its cafés, a mint tea or Turkish coffee can be nursed for hours as you watch other people hurry about their business. That's one of the joys of a holiday. If you're not worried about your lungs, try the hookah waterpipe known here as a *sheesha* or *narguileh*.

The glories of Alexandria's golden past under the Greeks or the more recent cosmopolitan community made famous by the novels of Lawrence Durrell are only a distant memory now. But romantics can track down the relics in the local museum or an old hotel bar. Around the harbour, the seafood restaurants and the nearby beaches make the visit worthwhile.

Luxor is a modern city that has grown up around the ancient temples of Karnak and Thebes. Beyond the monuments and fine museum, the bazaar is a good place to hunt down sculptures continuing the traditions of the ancient craftsmen.

At Aswan, famous both for the modern hydroelectric facilities of its dam and the ancient temples on its river islands, transport may take the more leisurely form of *calèches*—horse-drawn carriages—or cruises on graceful tall-sailed feluccas. The spice market here is as old as Egypt itself, and it's still the place for the ladies to find the best henna dye to add a red gleam to their hair. It is down around Luxor and Aswan that you will best appreciate the rich ethnic mix of the Egyptian people, descendants of the handsome black Nubians, Persians, Libyans, Turks and Mamelukes that have all contributed towards the nation's varied history.

The Resorts

For a complete change of pace from the sightseeing, you'll find at Hurghada on the Red Sea or Sharm El Sheikh and other resorts on the Sinai peninsula some of the world's best water sports and deepsea fishing facilities. And nothing to stop you enjoying the simpler pleasures of just lazing around on their fine sandy beaches.

Early morning or late afternoon when the sun has lost most of its heat, the hotels provide good tennis facilities. Many also organize camel or horseback safaris into the desert, and barbecues beneath the stars, with local Bedouin tribes providing food, fire and sometimes musical entertainment.

In Abydos temple, a deceased pharaoh presents his gifts to the gods.

Bernard Joliat

FLASHBACK

Egypt's ancient civilization has left a mark on mankind's imagination as fertile and invigorating as the Nile Valley's path through the desert. The earth's warm-up after the Ice Age had covered the land with tropical rainforest, but this dried out into the Sahara's arid wasteland, leaving only a few pockets of greenery at the oases and along the banks of the Nile river.

It was there that Stone Age hunters and fishermen settled to grow crops and rear cattle.

From about 3000 BC, their rulers, the pharaohs, united north (Lower) and south (Upper) Egypt into a single country. With its capital moving from Memphis (just south of modern Cairo) to Thebes (Luxor), Egypt became the dominant power in the eastern Mediterranean for the next 1,500 years. Rich farmland and the treasures of its craftsmen attracted invaders from Palestine, Libya and Persia. The Greeks and Romans followed and then a long succession of Byzantines, Arabs, Turks, British and French until independence was achieved in the 20th century. The conquerors come and go. The pyramids still stand, still inspiring awe in all who stand beneath them, still concealing secrets within their depths.

Hieroglyphics and Pyramids

In 3200 BC, the Egyptians developed their own system of hieroglyphics, at the same time as their trading partners in Mesopotamia (modern Iraq), were designing their cuneiform alphabet. The combination of pictorial and phonetic symbols served not only to record prayers, hymns and other religious texts, but also to draw up inventory for the grain harvests and accounts for business. The top scribe was the pharaohs' right-hand man. He combined his writing talents with those of high priest, doctor, astronomer, mathematician and architect. The most famous of them was Imhotep, who designed the first pyramid as a mausoleum for King Djoser at Saqqara, around 2680 BC. This stepped structure was followed by King Kheops' sheer-faced Great Pyramid at nearby Giza. It was a faithful reflection of the pyramidal political system in which the divine pharaoh was the pinnacle and the people who built it the base.

Golden Age of the Pharaohs

Scholars divide the pharaohs into 30 dynasties, lasting 2,700 years. The 18th and 19th dynasties, from about 1500 to 1200 BC, represent the heyday of their political power and artistic glory. They built the great temples of Luxor and Karnak and extended Egypt's empire northeast to Syria's modern border with Turkey, west into Libya and south into the Nubian kingdom that is now Sudan.

Queen Hatshepsut put on a false beard and made herself pharaoh. Her reign was one of peace and prosperity. The mystic pharaoh Akhenaton and his lovely Nefertiti did away with the dozens of traditional gods to worship just one, a radiation of the sun. Tutankhamun restored the old cult, though his main achievement was to die at 19 and become immortalized as the only pharaoh whose treasure survived the grave-robbers.

Ramses II was the greatest megalomaniac of them all, erecting gigantic monuments to himself throughout Egypt, most notably the colossal statues at Abu Simbel. But it was the beginning of the slow end to pharaonic greatness. He was most probably the pharaoh who let Moses' people go. The empire gradually shrank back to Egypt's national borders as it was invaded in turn by the Libyans, Assyrians and Persians.

From Alexander to Cleopatra

Alexander the Great arrived in 332 BC. Naturally, no world conquest could be complete without Egypt. The Macedonian warrior marched in from Palestine and had himself crowned pharaoh at Memphis. Out in the Western Desert, at the oasis of Siwa, a temple oracle assured him he was the son of Amun, the supreme creator-god. This morale-booster prompted him to set off to conquer India.

The Ptolemies who ruled after his death turned his capital, Alexandria, into the richest city of the ancient world. Cleopatra, the most illustrious of their monarchs, decided that if she could not beat Julius Caesar, she would seduce him. And then Mark Antony, too. For a brief shining moment, she shared with him control of the eastern half of Rome's empire. But their torrid affair ended in disaster in 30 BC. The Egyptian fleet was crushed by the Romans and the lovers committed suicide. Augustus Caesar reduced Egypt to a provincial backwater of the Roman Empire.

The First Christians

According to church tradition, the evangelist Mark preached Christianity in Alexandria during the 1st century AD. Egyptian Christians, known as Copts, founded the first monasteries, seeking refuge in the desert from Roman and later Byzantine persecution. The Copts, under the leadership of the Patriarch of Alexandria, were in constant theological and political conflict with the Greek Orthodox church, which was based in Constantinople.

The Byzantine emperors also ordered the closing and destruction of shrines still devoted to Egypt's ancient gods. The last holdout was the cult of Isis, which continued among Nubians down at Aswan until the reign of Emperor Justinian (AD 527–565).

After the Arab conquest of 641, the Copts who did not convert to Islam could claim, by avoiding intermarriage with the newcomers, the people's only unbroken link with their ancient Egyptian forefathers.

Islamic Rule

The desert nomad conquerors from Arabia had to reconcile their rough habits with the more sophisticated tastes of the Egyptians. It was left to Turks such as Ibn Tulun and the Fatimid dynasty from North Africa to bring a

Stunning sunsets. In **Aswan**, have a drink on the terrace of the grand old Cataract Hotel at the end of the afternoon, looking across at the white sails of the feluccas gliding past Elephantine Island. In **Luxor**, there's a similar old-fashioned joy to be had on the terrace of the Winter Palace, staring dreamily at the splendours of the Valley of the Kings. As a bonus, the ghost of Agatha Christie's Hercule Poirot may appear to solve another Death on the Nile.

hemis.fr/Frumm

new, specifically Islamic style to Egyptian life. The capital, a military garrison at the southern tip of the Delta, grew into the city of Cairo in 969. It developed to become the cultural centre of the Islamic world as the sheikhs kept on adding mosques, universities and palaces. The great Saladin (1171–93) repelled the Christian Crusaders and built Cairo's Citadel. The lusty warrior Mamelukes, raised from the level of

Wonderful nature spots. In the Gulf of Aqaba down at **Sharm El Sheikh,** the deep-sea fishing is superb and rare migrant birds gather at the neighbouring sanctuary of Ras Mohammed. On the Red Sea at **Hurghada** you can take a boat out both for fishing or bird-spotting around the offshore islands. In the Nile Valley, **Aswan** offers the best grounds for heron while vultures circle over the west bank.

slaves to sultans, divided their time between beautifying their city with wonderful stone carving and killing each other in palace intrigues.

The Ottoman Interlude

Things quietened down again with the advent of the Turks in 1517. Their Ottoman empire ruled Egypt with a loose, not to say indolent hand. The sultan did not interfere from Istanbul when rebellious Mamelukes competed with his Janissary warlords for control of the local Turkish pasha who was nominally in charge of

Egypt's affairs. For nearly three hundred years, the country stagnated.

Et Voilà Napoleon Bonaparte

The French army of Napoleon Bonaparte blew into Egypt like a desert whirlwind in 1798 and blew out again when routed by the British in 1801. But in between, they brought about a veritable revolution in Egypt's national consciousness, not with soldiers but with a company of 187 archaeologists, linguists, geographers, botanists and engineers. It was their pioneering excavations and research of Egyptian monuments and tombs which revealed to the world the full extent of the nation's ancient greatness. Their discovery of the Rosetta Stone, quickly confiscated by the British as the spoils of war, enabled a young French scholar, Jean-François Champollion, to break the cipher of hieroglyphics in 1822.

The 19th Century

Not quite light enough on his feet to float like a butterfly and sting like a bee (like his namesake the boxer, former Cassius Clay), Egypt's Mohammed Ali nevertheless proved a tough fighter when it came to asserting his country's autonomy vis-à-vis the Ottoman Turks. In 40 years government, he modernized the army and public education and streamlined the cotton industry and agriculture for export. But this upset European business interests. British gunboat diplomacy forced the Egyptians to content themselves with producing raw materials for Manchester; the French, meanwhile, smooth-talked Mohammed Ali's successors into granting them the concession to build and manage the Suez Canal in 1869.

When Egyptian colonels rebelled against this foreign interference with the preposterous slogan of "Egypt for the Egyptians", British troops stepped in. Henceforth, the Egyptian army was placed under British military command and the Egyptian ruler listened very hard to the advice of the British consul.

Monarchy and Independence

The British protectorate was formalized after World War I. In the face of the growing independence movement, Egypt became a constitutional monarchy, first under King Fuad, then Farouk. In World War II, the Western Desert was the theatre of Germany's push towards the Suez Canal, stopped by Montgomery's Allied forces at El Alamein.

Egypt's defeat in the Arab-Israeli War of 1948 precipitated the revolution led by Egyptian officers who ousted the playboy king Farouk four years later.

Wars and Peace

As president of the new republic, Gamal Abdel Nasser nationalized the Suez Canal in 1956, provoking an abortive Anglo-French raid as the Israelis attacked across the Sinai. Nasser's greatest triumph was the building of the Aswan Dam in 1964.

Soviet arms could not prevent a new debacle in the Six Day War of 1967 which left Israel occupying the Sinai peninsula. Anwar Sadat restored Egyptian self-confidence in the October War of 1973 by at least regaining control of the Suez Canal. Turning away from the Soviet Union to the United States, Sadat negotiated a peace treaty with Israel to retrieve the rest of the Sinai, but he was assassinated for his pains.

Into the New Century

Grappling with the economic problems of a huge population explosion, Sadat's successor Hosni Mubarak tried to pursue moderate policies in the face of fierce opposition from Muslim fundamentalists. After 30 years, his increasingly authoritarian rule was also challenged by ordinary protestors on the streets of Cairo, Alexandria, Suez and other cities, urging him to leave before the September elections. His trial for corruption and involvement in the death of peaceful protesters began in August 2011.

Silhouetted at sunset, the domes and minarets of El-Azhar Mosque.

Glen Allison

ON THE SCENE

In a nutshell, Egypt comprises the Nile Valley, the deserts, and two sea coasts on the Mediterranean and the Red Sea. Most visitors devote a large part of their time to the Nile Valley—Cairo and the Pyramids on its outskirts; the Upper Egypt region of Luxor and the Valley of the Kings over on the Nile's west bank; and further south, Aswan with a trip across the desert to Abu Simbel. But they can then also choose between the resorts of the Mediterranean coast, starting out from Alexandria, and those of the Red Sea around Hurghada. The Sinai alternative offers a combination of beach resorts, desert and mountains.

Cairo and the Pyramids

The metropolis is the hub not just of Egypt but of the whole Middle East. The noise and non-stop bustle of the capital don't perhaps encourage a prolonged stay, but there's no getting round it. You can't begin to understand Egypt without exploring the national museum and its Islamic quarters before going on your pilgrimage to the pyramids of Giza on the edge of town and further south to the Step Pyramid at Saqqara.

From one of the many rooftop bars or restaurants in the high-rise towers of the ultramodern hotels, you can take in the immense variety of the sprawling city. A tangle of urban highways, flyovers and avenues link and separate the skyscrapers of the business centre, the minarets and domes of the mosques and the steeple of an occasional Christian church. Two islands, Gezira and Roda, joined to the mainland by bridges, dominate the waters of the Nile. The boats wait there to take you on a cruise—or at least, from its quayside mooring, to serve you a dinner on the river.

Modern Cairo

Around the tumultuous Tahrir Square, the modern city shows the influence of three countries that played an important part in Egypt's development. Britain's mark can still be seen in some of the redbrick Victorian office buildings. The Egyptian Museum was originally a French creation, shops on Tala'at Harb and Qasr El Nil streets frequently have French names, and the second language on Arabic street signs is also French. The high-rise architecture and neon signs for soft drinks and fast food outlets are resolutely international.

Visitors from the US can be proud of the American University south of Tahrir Square—it has an excellent English bookshop if you are looking for serious literature on Egyptian culture.

Egypt reasserts its national pride at the Central Station, worth a visit even if you're not taking a train. This imposing structure crowned Egypt's entry into the modern railway age in 1851 with a service to Alexandria. Serious train spotters will enjoy the little Railway Museum at the back of the station. Founded in 1933, it displays scale models and real, historic trains, including the luxurious dining- and sleeping-cars of the Egyptian royal family.

Egyptian Museum

Dominating the north side of Tahrir Square is the Museum of Egyptian Antiquities. Only a tiny fraction of the more than 100,000 pieces of ancient Egyptian art can be exhibited in its halls, and even so it's impossible to get an overview on any one visit. But it is still a marvellous introduction to this mysterious civilization. It will help you appreciate all the more the wonders you will see at

Unmissable statues in the Egyptian Museum. Of all the hundreds of sculptures you will pass by on even the shortest visit to the Egyptian Museum, there are a few we think you would regret having missed—once you have seen the fabulous treasury of Tutankhamun, his golden chair and burial chambers. **King Djoser,** builder of Egypt's first pyramid at Saqqara, a noble carving in painted limestone (Archaic Period, 3rd Dynasty). **Khephren,** the pharaoh whose head appears on the great Sphinx at Giza, is seen here in gleaming black diorite stone, protected by a sacred falcon (Old Kingdom, 4th Dynasty). **Seneb the Dwarf** is sculpted in a charming family group with his wife and two children (Old Kingdom, 4th Dynasty). The hieroglyphic inscription tells us he was the pharaoh's wealthy wardrobe master. **Queen Nefertiti**—her name means "the beauty has come" and this head is felt by many to be at least the equal of the more famous sculpture in Berlin's Neues Museum (New Kingdom, 18th Dynasty).

the pyramids of Giza and Saqqara and the temples of Luxor, Aswan and Abu Simbel. A new visitor centre complete with bookstore, cafeteria, restaurant and a children's museum, an open-air exhibition on the east side of the museum, extension of opening times to 10 p.m., a new tour route and the removal of some of the collections to the Grand Egyptian Museum near the pyramids are all part of the ongoing Development Project.

The museum's star attraction is of course the treasure of Tutankhamun: the jewellery; the gold of his coffin and bejewelled death mask; even his gloves and sandals are made of gold. Nearby are the giant wooden burial chambers in which all these objects were stored to brighten up his afterlife. But leading up to this treasure trove of the 14th century BC are equally remarkable sculptures and paintings, not only of the pharaohs but also of the ordinary people of ancient Egypt—cooks, butchers, bakers, brewers—and beautifully depicted animals, birds and flowers, all in astonishingly vivid colours, considering they are 4,000–5,000 years old.

In the two mummy rooms on the first floor, you can see 27 famous pharaohs, among them Ramses II and Tuthmosis III, as well as members of the royal family and high priests.

Peeping parlours. In many of the grander mansions owned by pashas in the 17th and 18th centuries, you will notice on upper storeys closed balconies of finely crafted wooden lattice, known as mashrabiya. From these alcoves, the ladies of the house could watch the passers-by without running the unforgivable risk of being seen. Craftsmen continue the *mashrabiya* wood-carving tradition in the Khan El Khalili bazaar. If you don't want a whole alcove, you can settle for an ornate box or tray.

Islamic Cairo

Alongside the technological trappings of the modern city, Cairo continues to cultivate the age-old traditional life of its Islamic beginnings. Custom is timeless in Khan El Khalili's teeming bazaar, in the venerable mosques, great centres of learning as well as of worship, the Citadel, grand fortress of the sultans, even the medieval cemeteries, where the

istockphoto.com/Beesley

hemis.fr/Orteo

Michel Delanoe

hemis.fr/Orteo

living dwell side by side with their ancestors.

Tucked away behind the broad avenues and boulevards east of the city centre, the side streets and alleys of the old neighbourhoods invite you to explore. The aroma of barbecued lamb kebabs mixes with the haunting ballads of Oum Khalsoum, the nation's singing treasure, or the more recent pulsing rhythms of Arab rock music. No room for bus or taxi here, so wear your best walking shoes—but the kind that are easy to slip in and out of in case you have to go into a mosque.

Khan El Khalili

The Middle East's most celebrated bazaar has been here over 600 years. The stalls and workshops have passed from father to son, merchants and artisans of gold and silver, brass and glass, carpets and clothing, incense and spices, treasure and junk. It is indeed a favourite venue for tourists, but if you wish to get away from them, you can always duck down a side alley and find yourself among the hundreds of Egyptians who come here too.

View from the Citadel over the El Azhar Mosque and University. | Café Fishawi in Khan el-Khalili bazaar. | Citadel and Mohammed Ali Mosque. | Muslim women in the El Azhar Mosque.

Shopkeepers will offer you a coffee or mint tea. Accept it with a smile, as a gesture of friendship, not a trap for the unwary tourist. You really are not obliged to buy anything you don't want.

Qalawun Mosque
On Muizz li-Din Street, a main thoroughfare bordering Khan El Khalili, this mosque was built in the 13th century by a Mameluke sultan who began life as a Turkish slave. Brutally cruel to his rivals but great benefactor to the people, Qalawun included in the mosque a school for theological students and the city's first public hospital. In tribute to the architectural taste if not the faith of infidels, the buildings include a pair of Gothic windows he seized as booty from a Crusader church in Jerusalem and some pink granite columns taken from a pharaonic temple.

House of Beit Suhaymi
Behind the mansion's 17th-century façade are two pleasant gardens, one in the inner courtyard and the other beyond the main residential quarters. The dwelling was formed by joining together two merchant's houses and belonged to the Turkish dean of students at the city's El Azhar university. The men's quarters have fine wood carving in the *salamlik,* a reception room built around a marble fountain. The women's harem is decorated with cool turquoise tiles and marble floors.

El Azhar Mosque
Five minarets and six monumental gates mark this most prestigious of Cairo's mosques, housing a university revered throughout the Islamic world. Syrians, Moroccans and Turks have all studied here, each with a monumental gate leading to their separate living quarters. Entrance is at the Barber's Gate where students got their short-back-and-sides before classes. It takes you through to the mosque's huge central courtyard surrounded by ornate Persian-style arcades.

Bab Zuweila Gate
Topped by two onion-domed minarets that in fact belong to a neighbouring mosque, this familiar landmark of the old Islamic city was once its southern entrance. It was built in 1092. Under the Mamelukes and Turks, public executions were staged here and the heads were left for display on spikes. You can entertain more soothing thoughts in the shady garden of the El Muayyad mosque.

The Citadel
On the city's only piece of ground that rises any appreciable height above the plain, 75 m

Pharaonic village. The golden days of Pharaonic Egypt are vividly recreated in this theme park on an island a few miles from Cairo (3, Sharia El Bahr El Azam, Giza). You float along a network of canals in a barge, past the Pharaoh and his court, the pyramids, a marketplace and palace. The highlight is a replica of Tutankhamun's Tomb, faithfully reproduced down to the last detail, the only difference between this and the real tomb being the air-conditioning!

(246 ft), Sultan Saladin had this fortress built in 1176—by Crusader prisoners captured in Palestine. Its massive ramparts never had to resist foreign attack but were frequently subjected to the cannonballs of rival factions contesting the sultan's throne. Today, its silhouette is dominated by the domes and minarets of the Turkish-style mosque of Mohammed Ali, completed in 1857. Beside the cannons on the terrace behind the mosque, you get a great view across the medieval and modern quarters of the city. Don't let any guide fool you into believing that the Joseph's Well inside the Citadel precincts has anything to do with the Old Testament hero—it is named after Saladin, whose name was also Joseph (Yusuf).

Mosque of Sultan Hassan

Almost as imposing a fortress as the nearby Citadel, this great 14th-century shrine incorporates four theological schools and the sultan's mausoleum (though only Hassan's sons are buried there, since he disappeared without trace before the mosque was completed). The taller of its two minarets is the highest in Cairo, 86 m (282 ft). Its main prayer-hall has a splendid marble *mihrab,* an ornate niche set in the wall facing Mecca. Nearby is the *minbar* or pulpit, notable for its fine bronze door.

Museum of Islamic Art

The museum, resplendent after an 8-year renovation, is at the western edge of the old Islamic neighbourhoods, with an entrance on Bur Saïd Street. Its rich collections show how ingenious Islamic artists could be in their decorative style while respecting the religious taboo on painting or sculpting human or animal figures. Floral, geometric and "arabesque" motifs abound in furniture inlaid with mother of pearl, tortoise shell, as well as ceramics, glassware and gold and silver jewellery. Human beings manage to sneak into a few scenes of hunting and dancing by medieval Moroccan artists.

You will also notice here that the Mamelukes, besides being

formidable warriors, produced Egypt's most skilful sculptors of stone and wood since the age of the pharaohs.

Mosque of Ibn Tulun

If you have time or inclination to visit only one mosque, this could well be it. It is the city's oldest still standing (it was originally built in 879) and for many it is also the most elegant. According to legend, the mosque's sycamore wood beams came from Noah's Ark, brought here from Ararat. The outer walls are topped by fine stone tracery. Climb the external spiral staircase of the lovely Iraqi-style minaret for a great view of the old city.

Gayer-Anderson Museum

Adjacent to the Ibn Tulun mosque, this handsome house was transformed by its former owner, a British civil servant, into a museum showing how grandees of the Ottoman Empire lived in their heyday. Much of the furniture and ornament is exquisite. Visit the men's living room or *salamlik,* the women's harem, the secret closet from which the women watched the men, and the roof garden where they dined in summer.

Eastern Cemetery

Cairo's cemeteries are far from being morbid places devoted exclusively to mourning the dead. Egyptian Muslims have continued the custom of ancient pharaonic times of holding family reunions at the dearly departed's tomb, complete with weekend picnics. Add to that the houses, makeshift food-stalls and mini-markets that the city's homeless have installed more or less permanently among the tombs of their forefathers, and a place like the Eastern Cemetery becomes positively convivial. On the far side of the highway east of El Azhar university, the cemetery has as its landmarks two monumental domed mausoleums built by the great sultans, Barquq and Qaitbey.

The Pyramids

Of the Seven Wonders of the World only Egypt's pyramids have survived. Among all the world's great monuments, they have far and away the highest recognition factor. And yet, people seeing them up close for the first time cannot be blasé about them, however hard they try. It is only when you get close up that you appreciate the real size of the huge blocks of stone. The pharaohs built their pyramids to inspire awe, and 4,500 years later, it still works.

For a better understanding of the pharaohs who built them, try to fit in your visit to the Egyptian

Museum before going to the pyramids. A splendid new **Grand Egyptian Museum (GEM)** is undergoing construction near the Giza site; it is due to open in 2013. One of its prize exhibits will be the red granite statue of Ramses II which stood amidst the traffic fumes in the square outside Cairo Railway Station from 1954 to 2006 and is now being restored at Giza.

Giza

Built around 2600 BC, the celebrated trio of pyramids on the southern outskirts of Cairo have streamlined the step shape of Djoser's pyramid at Saqqara. The biggest is the **Great Pyramid of Kheops**, 137 m (450 ft) high, but, by an optical illusion, the narrower pyramid of Khephren built on higher ground looks taller. They stand on a limestone plateau, forming a royal cemetery to which the pharaohs' mummified bodies were transported from the Nile. Adjoining the pyramids are the remains of mortuary chapels where the mummies lay in state before being buried in chambers at the bottom of shafts dug deep into the pyramids.

Today, you can visit the pyramids on foot or on camel. Do not attempt to climb up the sides—it is not allowed, and there are plenty of guards around to make sure you obey. Guides will take you down to the burial chambers,

but you may find the effort through the cramped, narrow shaft, a trek taking up to 60 minutes, more strenuous than it is worth. If you do want to see inside, try **Khephren's pyramid** rather than that of Kheops. The trek is shorter and the pharaoh's red granite sarcophagus is still in the burial chamber.

Khephren's pyramid is also notable for the white limestone facing at the top. Originally all three pyramids had this smooth finish. It's said that the fine stone was removed in the Middle Ages to build houses in Cairo.

The third, more modest **pyramid of Mykerinus** was the last to be built here, reflecting a decline in the pharaohs' absolute power and money.

The Sphinx

With its lion's body and man's head but minus its nose and beard, this great mystic guardian of the pyramids continues to fascinate the pilgrims. The head is said to be that of Khephren. The nose did not drop off but was shattered by Mameluke Turks, using the monument for target practice—simultaneousely honouring the Islamic proscription against graven images. Over the centuries, the desert sands have often buried the Sphinx, almost to its head. Some 1,200 years after it was hewn from limestone, Tuthmosis IV left an inscribed tablet here telling how he dreamt the Sphinx had promised him he would become pharaoh only if he cleared away the sand. He obeyed.

Memphis

The pharaoh Menes founded Memphis, 28 km (17 miles) south of Giza, around 3000 BC. He is thought to have erected the temple of Ptah, while his son built the royal palace and made Memphis the first capital of Egypt. Thanks to the strategic position of the site, halfway between Upper and Lower Egypt and ideal for controlling trade, the city prospered, becoming the political and commercial centre of Egypt from the time of the Old Kingdom. It also had religious significance, with the country's biggest temples, and pharaohs were crowned here. During the New Kingdom (from around 1550 BC), Thebes took over as the centre of power. When El-Fustat (now Cairo) was built in the Middle Ages, Memphis was abandoned and its stones were used as building materials for Cairo houses. Only a few poignant ruins scattered

Barbara Ender

Bernard Joliat

The inscrutable gaze of the Sphinx, keeping watch in front of Khephren's pyramid. | A colourful papyrus reproducing ancient tomb paintings.

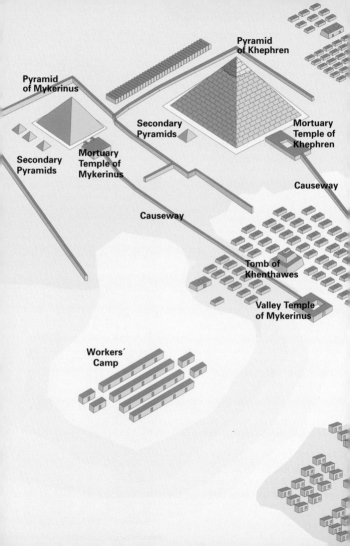

Pyramid
of Khephren

Pyramid
of Mykerinus

Secondary
Pyramids

Mortuary
Temple of
Khephren

Secondary
Pyramids

Mortuary
Temple of
Mykerinus

Causeway

Causeway

Tomb of
Khenthawes

Valley Temple
of Mykerinus

Workers´
Camp

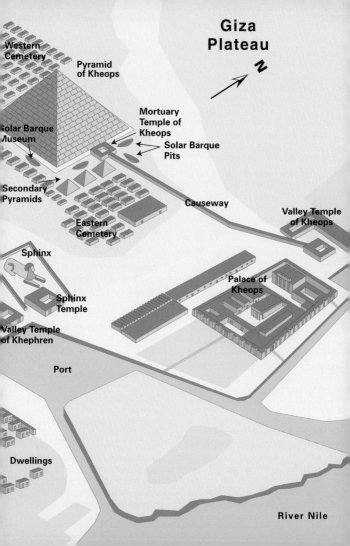

But what does it mean? It is generally agreed that the purpose of the pyramids was both religious and political. Each gigantic edifice of limestone and granite was conceived as a royal tomb, with the burial chamber hidden deep in the bowels of the pyramid. To conform to the ritual of the sun-cult, the pyramid stands precisely four-square, so that its east and west sides catch the direct rays of the sun when it rises and when it sets. But the overwhelming form and mass also reflect the absolute power of the pharaoh—at the pinnacle—over the people who built it for him—at the base.

istockphoto.com/Rihak

around the fields remain from the splendid royal palace, the garrison with its arsenal and fleet, the temples and necropolis. However, you can see a giant statue of Ramses II (1279–1213 BC), now reclining beneath a shelter. It stood 13 m (43 ft) tall, probably in front of the temple of Ptah. The red granite statue of Ramses II moved from Cairo to Giza in 2006 also came from Memphis. An alabaster sphinx, in fairly good condition and with an inscrutable smile, was discovered in 1912. It weighs 80 tonnes and measures 8 m (26 ft) in length and over 4 m (13 ft) in height.

Saqqara

The necropolis of pyramids surrounded by the smaller tombs of nobles stands on a desert plateau west of the vanished royal capital of Memphis—the west, where the sun sets, being the Land of the Dead. Many of the pyramids have been reduced by time and the elements to little more than piles of rubble, but the most important, King Djoser's mausoleum, still stands proudly intact. His is not only the first of the pyramids (around 2670 BC) but the world's earliest known monument to be built of stone rather than brick. It won for its designer, the high priest Imhotep, world renown as the father of architecture.

To get to the **Step Pyramid**, you pass through a stone-walled precinct. In the corridor and side chambers, stone is used to imitate wooden beams and bundles of reeds lashed together to form columns. At the end of a broad courtyard, the pyramid rises in six tiers. The pharaoh's burial chamber (off-limits to all but professional archaeologists) lies at the bottom of a shaft cut into the bedrock beneath the pyramid, with other chambers for his family further down.

Not far from the Step Pyramid, courtiers were buried in tombs known as *mastaba,* an Arab word for their bench-like shape. Inside are delightful carved friezes of everyday life in ancient Egypt—harvest, hunting, boat-building—the netherworld being conceived as continuing business as usual. Two of the best tombs belonged to Mereruka, a royal chamberlain, and Princess Idut.

Do not miss the **Imhotep Museum**, devoted to discoveries from the area, including sarcophagi, statues, friezes, ships, mummies and ornaments.

Dahshur

Eleven pyramids were built here, 15 km (9 miles) south of Saqqara, during the Old and Middle kingdoms. Until 1996, the area around the site was a military zone. The most interesting structure is the Bent Pyramid, built under pharaoh Snoferu, father of Kheops. About halfway up, the angle changes from 55 to 43 degrees: maybe the architect changed his plans in order to speed up the work or save on building materials. The Red Pyramid also dates from Snoferu's time. It is over 100 m (328 ft) high, with a base 220 m (722 ft) square. Its core was cased in Tura limestone; inscriptions were found on the backs of many pieces, including Snoferu's cartouche and the names of work gangs left for posterity in red paint.

Getting ready for eternity. To make sure these pyramidal tombs were finished in time for their death, the pharaohs had to start building them as soon as they came to the throne. That gave Kheops at the most 23 years, 2606–2583 BC, to build the Great Pyramid. It consists of more than 2 million blocks, an average of 240 blocks a day, averaging 2.5 tons each, to be quarried, dressed and put into place. The rough stone for the inner filling was found on the Giza plateau, but finer white limestone had to be ferried across the Nile from the quarries of Tura, while the best quality granite for the burial chambers and sarcophagus had to be shipped downriver from Aswan. Modern engineers have estimated the labour force to consist of 4,000 men at any one time—including boatmen, quarry-workers, building-labourers and masons. And no unions.

iStockphoto.com/
De Mattos

The main entrance to the temple of Luxor is overwhelming.

Mickael David

Luxor

Determined by the course of the Nile, the southern part of the country is known as Upper Egypt. At its heart are Luxor and Karnak, which together formed Thebes, the national capital at the height of the empire, around 1500 BC. Here are the great temples. Across the river on the west bank, carved out of the rock in the Valley of the Kings, are the tombs of the pharaohs, where the treasure of Tutankhamun was discovered. Excursions north and south of Luxor take you to other major sanctuaries built by the pharaohs and by their Greek and Roman successors.

But Upper Egypt also gives you a close-up view of rural life in the Nile Valley. On the river early in the morning, from your cruise boat or felucca, you will see white-clad farmers or their little boys riding donkeys past the minaret of the village mosque to the green fields of sugar cane, corn or cotton. Wife and daughter prepare a bean-stew outside the mudbrick houses or wash clothes down by the river. To irrigate the fields, some of the water-pumps have electric motors, but most are much the same as those depicted on frescoes in the tombs of the pharaohs.

Its name comes from the Arabic El Uqsor (palaces), temples being regarded in the Middle East as the palaces of the gods. The riverside town has grown up around the tourist industry since the 19th century, but beyond the hotels, it has quickly taken on the aspect of a traditional Egyptian community. Side by side with the Tourist Bazaar for souvenirs and craftwork is the more lively townspeople's bazaar selling fruit, vegetables, spices and household goods. The best way to get around town, whether visiting the temples or markets, is by taxi (agree on a price beforehand). The horse-drawn *calèches* are picturesque but often a rip-off.

Temple of Luxor

The great sanctuary dedicated principally to the creator-god, Amun, runs parallel to the river. Its ceremonial entrance is at the north end, where it was linked to Karnak 3 km (2 miles) to the north by the monumental **Avenue of Sphinxes**, recently restored. Only one of the two original obelisks stands at the huge twin gate-tower known as a pylon—the other now stands on Place de la Concorde in Paris. The colossal statues are of Ramses II, also depicted on the pylon as a warrior, but the temple itself was largely the work of Amenhotep III, a century earlier around 1350 BC. Ramses was a deft hand at appropriating ancestors' monuments for his own glory.

Karnak: Amun Temple Enclosure

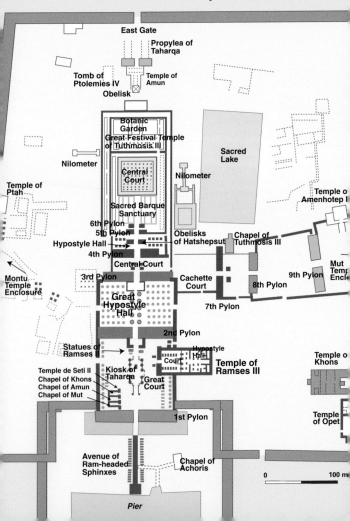

East Gate

Propylea of Taharqa

Tomb of Ptolemies IV

Temple of Amun

Obelisk

Botanic Garden

Great Festival Temple of Tuthmosis III

Nilometer

Central Court

Sacred Lake

Nilometer

Temple of Ptah

Sacred Barque Sanctuary

Temple of Amenhotep I

6th Pylon

5th Pylon

Hypostyle Hall

Obelisks of Hatshepsut

Chapel of Tuthmosis III

4th Pylon

Central Court

Montu Temple Enclosure

3rd Pylon

Cachette Court

Mut Temple Enclosure

8th Pylon

9th Pylon

7th Pylon

Great Hypostyle Hall

2nd Pylon

Statues of Ramses II

Hypostyle Hall

Temple de Seti II

Chapel of Khons

Chapel of Amun

Chapel of Mut

Kiosk of Taharqa

Court

Temple of Ramses III

Temple of Khons

Great Court

1st Pylon

Temple of Opet

Avenue of Ram-headed Sphinxes

Chapel of Achoris

0   100 m

Pier

Amenhotep gets his due in the hypostyle hall of 32 columns where carvings show him paying tribute to the creator-god of whom he was declared to be the offspring. In one of the courtyards leading to the hall, you may be surprised to see the minaret and dome of a mosque. It was built, long before the temple was excavated, to honour Abu El Haggag, a revered Muslim holy man of the 12th century, on the ruins of a Coptic church, which was incorporated into the temple walls. So for centuries this has been a holy place for many faiths.

Luxor Museum

The waterfront museum is housed in a handsome modern building, beautifully displayed and lit. Open for late afternoon and evening viewing, it is a good idea to visit it after the temples for a moment of quiet contemplation. Its collection of recent findings include splendid statues of the temple-builders, Amenhotep III and Tuthmosis III, a sphinx of Tutankhamun, and fascinating wall-paintings of Akhenaten and his wife, Nefertiti.

Heritage Centre

In the Mubarak Library, this cultural centre opened in 2007. Its Panorama of Culture is an interactive showcase documenting Egypt's rich history. There is also

Obelisks overseas. Egypt's 19th-century ruler Mohammed Ali found he could attract foreign investment by giving away obelisks. France's King Louis-Philippe big-heartedly gave an ornamental clock in exchange for the monument standing in the Place de la Concorde in Paris. Britain's Cleopatra's Needle came from the Heliopolis sanctuary near Cairo, but lay for 50 years in Alexandria before anybody could figure a way of getting it to the Thames Embankment. New York's needle in Central Park is also from Heliopolis, but it's suffering badly from pollution.

istockphoto.com/Walton

a 3-D display of the pyramids and archaeological excavations, and astrological exhibits.

Karnak

On the northern edge of Luxor, the sprawling complex grouping several temples within its precincts is the most imposing of all of ancient Egypt's many sanctuaries. Over the centuries, it grew to its present vast proportions as one dynasty after the other added its own shrine or monument. It's an appropriate site for the spectacular evening Sound and Light show narrating the glory of the pharaohs.

At the Karnak end of the Avenue of Sphinxes, the figures have ram's heads, unlike the human-headed sphinxes of Luxor. An effigy of the creator-god Amun was carried along the avenue on a sacred boat from the river in the ceremonies linking the Karnak and Luxor temples.

Karnak's monumental centre-piece is the Great Hypostyle Hall of 134 giant columns arranged in 16 rows. Two sets of carved reliefs on the columns and the walls show the pharaohs, Seti I and his son Ramses II, making offerings to the gods and defeating their enemies in battle. The worshippers—priests, royal family and nobles only—gathered in the hall before the pharaoh paid private tribute to the gods in the inner sanctuary.

Beyond the hall is the obelisk of Tuthmosis I, then you come to the pink granite obelisk of Hatshepsut, who served as regent for her stepson and also took over as pharaoh, putting on man's clothing and a ceremonial beard to bolster her position in those anti-feminist times. Outside the main temple buildings is the Sacred Lake on which a communion of the gods was enacted in boats. It is also the setting for the climax of the Sound and Light show.

Theban Necropolis

The royal cemetery has an awesome setting in the valleys of desert crags over on the west bank. The pharaohs and their courtiers were ferried across from the city of Thebes and entombed deep underground behind unobtrusive entrances, to discourage grave-robbers. Unsuccessfully—with the exception of Tutankhamun.

You, too, will be ferried across from Luxor (or taken by minibus) and be guided to a few of the best and most representative tombs and mortuary temples where the deceased were prepared for burial. Literally hundreds of tombs are scattered around the desert hills, so don't expect to visit more than five or six on a half-day visit. Besides the taxis, you can rent horses, camels or bicycles.

Valley of the Kings

There are currently 63 tombs accounted for in this most famous region of the Theban necropolis, and digging still goes on. Even without the treasure, there is plenty to see. Thanks to the dry desert climate, the tomb-decorations are astoundingly well-preserved—vividly carved and brightly painted scenes of religious rituals and the everyday world. The scenes depict the good things of life that the deceased pharaoh will need in the

Theban Necropolis

N ←

Carter's House

Site of Ramesside Temple

Temple of Seti I

Temple of Tuthmosis III

Temple of Tuthmosis III

Ramesseum

Deir el-Bahari Temple of Hatshepsut

El-Sheikh Abd el-Gurnah

Mortuary Temple of Merenptah

Colossi of Memnon (Amenhotep III)

Tomb of Amenhotep III

VALLEY OF THE KINGS

Tombs of the Kings

Tomb of Tutankhamun

Temple of Mentuhotep II

Ptolemaic Temple

Deir el-Medinah

Site of Temple of Amenhotep III

Ticket Office

Tombs of the Queens

VALLEY OF THE QUEENS

Medinet Habu

Site of Palace of Amenhotep III

KARNAK

RIVER NILE

LUXOR

THEBAN NECROPOLIS

Villagers near Luxor paint their family history and travels on their house façades.

afterlife—household servants, fruits of the harvest, fishing and hunting, games for moments of leisure. Some tombs still have granite coffins in the burial chamber. The royal mummies have been restored and placed on display in Cairo's Egyptian Museum, except for Tutankhamun, who lies in his tomb, encased in an air-conditioned plexiglass box. Just his head and feet are visible. Scanner analysis in 2005 showed that he probably died from gangrene after an accident.

Queen Hatshepsut's Temple

The queen who made herself pharaoh chose the most spectacular site in which to build her mortuary temple. Dedicated to Amun and the cow-headed goddess Hathor, the temple in which the mummified queen was to lie in state rises on three colonnaded terraces cut into the hillside to the inner sanctuary at the top. On the carved reliefs of the queen's birth, paying tribute to the gods and her trade expeditions to other African kingdoms, Hatshepsut's image has been systematically obliterated by her jealous successors, Tuthmosis II and III and Amenhotep IV.

Ramesseum

The sprawling precincts of the Ramesseum contained both a mortuary temple and residence for the pharaoh's ceremonial visits to the west bank. Beside battle scenes of Ramses II's valour against the Hittites, his black granite statue lies in fragments, once standing 17 m (55 ft) high and weighing over 1,000 tons.

Colossi of Memnon

Still proudly intact, the two colossi sit in solitary splendour at the edge of green cornfields, gazing implacably towards the rising sun. They once guarded the entrance to the mortuary temple of Amenhotep III. These sandstone giants, 17 m (56 ft) high, were the only monuments still visible when the French began excavations in the 19th century.

North of Luxor

Downriver over on the west bank of the Nile, two major sanctuaries in picturesque rural settings can be visited as part of a single day-trip.

Abydos

The temples are located amid green fields of sugar cane and barley against a backdrop of the Western Desert hills 150 km (93 miles) north of Luxor. The Abydos sanctuary was a centre of pilgrimage where pharaohs and commoners worshipped the na-tionally revered earth-god Osiris. Seti I, the pharaoh who built the main temple, is portrayed there in mummified form identifying him with Osiris, lord of the netherworld. Once again, as at Luxor, Seti's son Ramses II tried to appropriate the place for himself, though his temple is smaller and plainer than that of Seti I. The sanctuary includes the Osireion, a mausoleum for the god's remains.

Pilgrims wanted to be buried close to Osiris; as an alternative they could buy small mass-produced statues inscribed with their name and title to leave there, associating them with the deity who protected mankind in the afterlife.

Worth the candle. The men who uncovered Tutankhamun's treasure, more than 3,000 years after it was buried with the 19-year-old king, had no idea it was there. They didn't even have an inkling of his identity. British artist Howard Carter had been pottering around Egypt for 30 years, sketching the ruins for archaeologists and rich American tourists.

He was convinced there was some treasure somewhere in those hills, but drew a blank every time he dug. In 1922, after seven years of excavation financed by amateur Egyptologist Lord Carnarvon, he explored the tomb of Ramses VI, again to no avail, until he came across a stairway leading down to another tomb next door. Scrabbling through the rubble with the good lord breathing down his neck, Carter made a hole big enough to peer through with a candle. "Can you see anything?" asked Carnarvon. "Yes," said Carter, "Wonderful things."

Denderah

The Temple of Hathor here is best visited on the way back from Abydos to Luxor in time for the wonderful sunset view from the rooftop. Built by the Greek Ptolemies and completed under Roman rule in AD 64, this shrine is among the best preserved of Egyptian temples. Recent restoration has revealed magnificent colours in the frescoes. On the courtyard columns, florid Corinthian capitals have replaced the simpler Egyptian papyrus-bloom shapes, and hieroglyphs identify emperors Augustus, Nero and Claudius among the temple's benefactors. On the ceiling of the hypostyle hall, astrology buffs can check signs of the zodiac assimilated to Egyptian deities, notably Osiris as Leo, and his sister Isis as Virgo. Early Egyptian Christians equated Isis with the Virgin Mary.

South of Luxor

River cruises have made the region between Luxor and Aswan a major part of their itinerary, but also popular are road excursions through the Nile Valley as it narrows on its way to the Nubian south. The people here are more pronouncedly African, often inhabiting villages relocated from those submerged by the waters of the Aswan High Dam. A trio of temple sanctuaries were in large part restored by the Alexandria-based Ptolemies to assert their authority over Upper Egypt. They were frequently devoted to popular animal cults.

The most fascinating royal tombs. Many of the tombs are not open to the public. The following can be visited, with numbering from the maps available at the ticket office. **Ramses III** (11) is famous for the frescoes of harpists singing the king's praises, as well as a cook preparing a banquet. **Amenhotep II** (35) is among the deepest, with 90 stairs down to the superb carved reliefs in the burial chamber, together with the king's sarcophagus. **Tuthmosis III** (34) is worth the climb for the splendid rounded oblong burial chamber and its handsome red sandstone sarcophagus. In the tomb of **Nakht** (52), a scribe and astronomer, paintings show him with his wife, banqueting and making offerings; detailed harvest scenes. In that of **Ramose** (55), governor of Thebes, a procession of mourners wear transparent robes. The mummy of **Tutankhamun** (62) is displayed in a plexiglass case.

TOMB OF
TUT ANKH AMON
NO: 62

Esna

Barely an hour's drive from Luxor, the temple of the ram-headed god Khnum lies in a bizarre location, now a hollow 9 m (30 ft) below the ground level of the town of Esna. Over the centuries, houses have grown up around and above the sacred site. Some of them still cover an unexcavated part of the temple.

The imposing 24-column hypostyle hall was erected by Emperor Tiberius. He and other Roman rulers chose to be depicted in traditional pharaonic poses smiting Egypt's enemies or honouring the deities. On the paving of the temple courtyard are the graffiti left by Napoleon Bonaparte's soldiers who passed through here in 1798.

Edfu

About 50 km (30 miles) further south from Esna, the town's beautifully preserved Temple of Horus has a pylon second in size only to that of the great sanctuary at Karnak. It took the Ptolemies more than a century to build the temple, incorporating much of the masonry of earlier ones. The falcon representing the god Horus is ever-present, most notably in a black granite statue in the courtyard. On the carved reliefs in the two hypostyle halls and on the walls surrounding the inner sanctuary you can see the great national rituals celebrated in connection with the Edfu temple. In a carnival atmosphere among villagers on the river banks, an effigy of the goddess Hathor left Denderah north of Luxor each year on a grand two-week cruise to reenact her marriage with Horus at Edfu. Other friezes show the falcon-headed Horus vanquishing the evil Seth, portrayed as a crocodile or hippopotamus. In the temple surroundings you will see many other carvings representing processions and illustrations of the legend of Horus.

Kom Ombo

Closer to Aswan than Luxor, the Kom Ombo sanctuary commands an enchanting site on a mound above the river bank. It is in fact a double temple, divided into shrines for Sobek the crocodile-god on one side and Haroeris, one of the old forms of Horus, on the other. It was probably intended as a sanctuary for the reconciliation of these traditionally hostile forces of light and darkness. Their images abound in the carved reliefs. Hundreds of crocodiles used to gather on a sandbar near Kom Ombo to mate or just sunbathe until the steamboats drove them all away in the 19th century. Their mummified ancestors can be seen stored in one of the temple's chapels.

There's nothing more relaxing than a felucca trip along the Nile.

hemis.fr / Frumm

The South

The southern border with Sudan, cutting through the ancient kingdom of Nubia, has historically been Egypt's rampart and gateway to the rest of Africa. It was here that the pharaohs established their trading post in the market town of Aswan, a military garrison on Elephantine Island and their mightiest monuments at Abu Simbel.

The desert plateau is rose-tinted and ochre. These are the colours of the coveted granite which, along with the alabaster quarried around for the finer sculptures, the pharaohs shipped downriver to Luxor, Saqqara and Giza for their monuments. Aswan granite is still much sought after for modern office buildings and hotels.

It is here that Egypt's greatest feat of engineering since the pyramids, the Aswan High Dam, has marshalled the flow of the Nile and created the huge Lake Nasser reservoir to give the country's farmland a balanced supply of water, and most of the nation's electricity.

Aswan

The balmy climate makes it a delightful place in which to wind down from the hectic pace of any journey around Egypt. Besides visiting the monuments, spare time just to hang around, stroll along the river or glide around its islands in a felucca. And rub shoulders with the culturally distinctive Nubian community.

The Town

In ancient Egyptian the name Aswan means "market". Start at the Bazaar along Sharia El Suk (Market St). Among the phials of perfumes and sacks of spices are the fragrancy and colours of the town itself. The tourist souvenir stalls are at the north end. And at the end of your sightseeing day, take a stroll along the Corniche riverfront promenade for an enchanting view of the islands and the feluccas.

Nubia Museum

With exhibits on three floors, this fascinating museum displays 3,000 artefacts tracing the cycles of Nubian civilization from prehistory to modern times: fossils, rock drawings, a monumental statue of Rameses II, heads of pharaohs in pink and black granite, mummies, tomb paintings and reliefs. An outdoor section devoted to the daily lives of the Nubians contains a stone tomb and typical mud houses.

The Islands

The islands, midstream rocks and sandbars together make up the First Cataract, most northerly of half a dozen breaking up the flow of the Nile. As you cruise among them, spare a few piastres for the little boys paddling around in tiny box-boats and singing snatches of English, French or German folksongs, according to your nationality.

The temples of Isis on what is now called **New Philae Island** were saved by modern engineers and archaeologists from flooding by the Aswan High Dam. The temples were moved from the original Philae Island to nearby Agilika, which was painstakingly reshaped to resemble the original Philae as much as possible.

The shrines and gateways span six centuries from the last of the pharaohs through the Greek Ptolemies to the Roman emperors. Isis was undoubtedly the most cherished of Egyptian goddesses and, as inscriptions on Philae from AD 452 show, the last to resist the bans of Christianized Rome. As sound and light shows go, the Giza pyramids or Karnak temple may be spectacular, but the story of Isis and the charming island setting make the Philae show much more romantic.

The military garrison made palm-covered **Elephantine Island** originally more important than the mainland town. Its ruined temple was dedicated to Khnum, ram-headed protector of the Nile's sources. The two museums are worth visiting. One is very modern; the other, more old-fashioned was founded in 1902. It is set in the villa of the designer of the first Aswan dam and exhibits, among other interesting items, a mummified ram and a gold bust of Khnum.

The smaller **Kitchener Island** was given to the grand old imperial British soldier for his exploits in Sudan in 1896–98. It's a cool and pleasant garden of tropical plants and trees complete with teahouse for late afternoon excursions. It is also known as Botanical Island.

Aswan High Dam

Amidst all the relics of ancient Egypt, it is worth taking time out to visit the country's great modern technological achievement south of town. A highway runs across the top of the dam past a hydroelectric plant to an observation deck in the middle, overlooking Lake Nasser. The Soviet-Egyptian cooperation that built it deserved something better than the ghastly gigantic monument at the west end of the dam.

The Quarries

Aswan's granite and alabaster quarries were as important to the pharaohs' architects and sculptors as the marble quarries of Carrara in Italy were to Michelangelo. Just south of town, in the Northern Quarries, you can clamber around a red granite obelisk abandoned in its trench 3,500 years ago because it developed a fatal crack. Other unfinished ancient monuments and carvings can be seen in the Southern Quarries, including a mummy-shaped colossus lying on its back and stone coffins intended for the Ptolemies but somehow never delivered back up in Alexandria.

Mickael David

Feluccas on the Nile near Aswan. | **One of the temples of Isis, moved to Agilika Island, reshaped to resemble the original Philae and renamed New Philae.**

hemis.fr/Maisant

Mausoleum of Aga Khan

On the Nile's west bank facing the southern tip of Elephantine Island is a hilltop edifice honouring the memory of the Aga Khan (1877–1957). This man of legendary wealth heading the Ismaili Muslims of Pakistan and east Africa chose the gentle climate of Aswan to soothe his aches and pains in winter. Overlooking the family's white palace, the terrace of the pink granite mausoleum affords a grand view of Aswan and its islands. Every day, a fresh red rose is placed on the Aga Khan's marble sarcophagus in the mausoleum, first by his widow, then, after her death in 2000 by the gardener. The mausoleum is not open to the public.

Abu Simbel

The enthroned colossi of Ramses II sit right on the Sudan border. In the 13th century BC, their formidable presence was a political statement asserting the pharaoh's dominion over these southern regions. The two temples they guard also served as treasure houses to store gold brought from Nubia prior to shipment downriver to Luxor and the Delta. For centuries, they lay almost buried in the sands and oblivion until a Swiss traveller, Johann Burckhardt, rediscovered them in 1813.

Raising Abu Simbel. It may seem crazy enough to have cut the temples and statues into more than a thousand pieces and moved them one by one to safety. But compare that with other ideas seriously considered: one was to leave the temples where they were, but protected by a counter-dam that would have cost as much as the Aswan High Dam itself. Another was to enclose them in a glass bubble and let tourists visit them underwater. The Americans suggested cutting the two temples out of their hillside each in one gigantic piece and floating them downriver on a pontoon to the new site.

As it was, the Swedish, French, German and Italian consortium took four years and $40 million to do the job. The temples' journey was just 65 m (213 ft) uphill and 210 m (688 ft) back from the river. There, they were inserted in two new dome-shaped "mountains" of concrete covered with natural rock. The domes were precisely oriented to respect the sanctuary's original ritual effect of the rising sun penetrating the inner shrine at a particular time of year, calculated to be February 21 and October 21.

Michel Delanoe

The temples were cut from the sandstone rock sloping down to the river. In 1964, when the Aswan High Dam was due to turn this stretch of the river into the huge Lake Nasser, modern technological genius dismantled and moved them to dry ground 65 m (210 ft) higher up and 200 m (650 ft) back from the river.

From Aswan, Abu Simbel is 45 minutes' flight (the airfield was specially built for the new temple complex) or a four-hour drive—when you may see a bedouin camel caravan heading to or from Sudan. Either way, even if it means setting off for the drive in the middle of the night, try to get there in the early morning when the sun is low in the east, highlighting the statues.

Temple of Ramses II

All four colossi on the façade of the temple are of Ramses II himself, or perhaps we should say Himself, as he is portrayed as the sun-god, supreme Egyptian deity, seated to face the rising sun. Ancient Egypt's most extravagant statement of imperial vanity, the statues stand 20 m (65 ft) high. The royal insignia include the *nemes,* a head cloth, with a sacred cobra on his brow, double crown of Lower and Upper Egypt, and a false beard. Above the statues in the middle, almost as an afterthought, is a statue of Re-Herakhty, until then traditional effigy of the sun-god. An earthquake has toppled the head and torso of one of the four Ramses statues and they still lie at its feet. On the two left-hand statues, you may spot on the legs graffiti left by Greek and Phoenician mercenaries. Just as humble as Re-Herakhty are small statues of the wife and children Ramses deigned to include in the monument. Right at the top, a line of baboons are praying to the rising sun.

Inside the temple is a classical hypostyle hall, with more colossi of Ramses II standing against the columns, with carved reliefs and paintings of his battle triumphs. At the back is the inner shrine to which only the pharaoh had access—and the sun.

Temple of Nefertari

The very existence of this sanctuary here is in itself a mark of the pharaoh's exceptional respect for the best-beloved of his wives. She, too, is deified and given colossi equal in size to those of her husband—though four of his flank just two of hers. Inside, the cow-eared heads on the pillars of the hypostyle hall show the temple is dedicated to the goddess Hathor. In the carved reliefs, Ramses pays courteous homage to his wife and even lets her go with him to battle.

Red sky over the Red Sea in the region near Hurghada.

Huber/Huber

Red Sea

The colour of the water is normally deep blue-green, but the dye from algae sometimes turns the sea reddish-brown, hence the name. For swimmers, the good news is that it has some of the warmest seawater in the world.

Suez Canal

For some, the canal may be the gateway to the Red Sea coast. Linking the Mediterranean to the Indian Ocean, it's a kingpin in Egypt's international trade. It has made a dramatic recovery since the 1978 peace treaty with Israel.

Port Said

The town was founded in the 19th century in association with the building of Suez Canal. After undergoing considerable war damage, the city has been pleasantly reconstructed and is now one of the world's major ports. The bustle around the harbour can be a raucous introduction to modern Egypt. All the time-honoured techniques of the medieval bazaar are applied to the free-zone's market in electronic goods from Japan and Korea. More seriously, the town museum has a remarkable collection of pharaonic, Greco-Roman, Coptic and Islamic art.

Countering the military humiliations of 1956 and 1967, Egypt commemorates its successes of the 1973 war in a Military Museum on the seafront promenade. You may wish to take a ferry across the canal to visit the new suburb of **Port Fouad** on the East or Asian bank.

Ismailiya

Founded in 1860 by Pasha Ismail, the town of 300,000 has a certain faded colonial charm about it, dating from the days of its French and British canal-managers. The villas are surrounded by pleasant gardens of bougainvillea and groves of pines, eucalyptus trees and poplars, planted when the city was founded. To the southeast of town, **Lake Timsah** (Crocodile) provides beaches and lazy fishing.

Where did they cross? Did the Hebrews really follow Moses across the Red Sea? Did the waters ever part anywhere but in Cecil B. De Mille's *Ten Commandments* basin at Paramount Studios in Hollywood? Or was it all just a leap of faith? A Californian team of archaeologists and geologists say that if it did happen, the most likely spot was the northern end of the Red Sea, in the Bitter Lakes marshlands around the Suez Canal.

Suez City

Majestically guarding the southern end of the great waterway, Suez City is lapped by the warm waters of the Gulf of Suez. It has recovered well from frequent bombing in the Arab-Israeli wars, with green parkland and new beaches along Suez Bay.

Port Tawfiq is a good place to watch freighters coming in and out of the canal from Asia, Africa and the Americas. A forlorn-looking pedestal there no longer has its statue of canal-builder Ferdinand de Lesseps, knocked off after the Anglo-French invasion of 1956.

Resorts

Holiday resorts on the coast from the Suez Canal to the Sudanese border are fast developing as places to unwind in after a spell of strenuous sightseeing among the monuments of the Nile Valley. Relax your mind and stretch your muscles with some leisurely snorkelling, casual fishing and, for the more ambitious, great deep-sea diving among the coral. Or just relax everything by doing nothing on a fine sandy beach.

Ain Sukhna

Its proximity to Cairo, just 55 km (34 miles) south of Suez makes this resort a popular day trip or weekend stay away from the capital. Its attractions include fine beaches and state-of-the-art water sports facilities with which to explore the coral reefs. Ain Sukhna is Arabic for "hot spring", derived from nearby sulphur springs originating in the Gebel Ataka mountain.

Zafarana

This small community 62 km (39 miles) south of Ain Sukhna serves principally as a gateway-town for visitors heading for the ancient monasteries of St Anthony and St Paul. Believed to be the oldest in Egypt (4th century), they are tucked away in the Red Sea mountains. Their heyday was from the 12th to 15th centuries, before being plundered by Bedouins. Each has several brightly frescoed churches, along with mill, bakery and library. Library manuscripts include ancient Coptic versions of the liturgy and an epistle of St Paul.

El Gouna

Built on clusters of islands surrounded by lagoons, El Gouna lies 20 km (12 miles) north of Hurghada. From its beginnings as a small marina, it has grown into an exclusive resort with fine beaches, renowned hotels and a developing town, carefully engineered to fit harmoniously into the environment. The heart of town, set on an island, is the Kafr, with restaurants, bars and clubs, a

SUEZ CANAL

One of the most famous waterways in the world, it extends for 195 km 117 miles) from Port Said on the Mediterranean to Port Suez on the Red Sea, reducing the route from Western Europe to India by almost 8,000 km (5,000 miles) The canal differs in width from one end to the other; at the northern end, it is 315 m (1,033 ft) wide at the surface and 215 m (918 ft) on the canal bed, while the southern entrance is narrower: 280 m (918 ft) on the surface, 195 m (640 ft) on the bed. In contrast with the Panama Canal, the Suez has no locks and is navigable for vessels with a draught of up to 16 m (53 ft). Passage through the canal takes about 14 hours; it is used annually by some 15,000 ships. Altogether, they transport 14 per cent of worldwide cargo carried by sea. The canal is an important source of revenue for Egypt, bringing in around $3.5 billion each year.

Ramses II (1298–1235 BC) was the first to attempt construction of a freshwater canal joining Lake Timsah (near present-day Ismailia) to the Nile. Then, towards 600 BC, pharaoh Necho II added a section from Timsah to the Red Sea. An oracle put a stop to the work which is said to have killed some 120,000 men. Persia's Darius I completed the work. Roman emperor Trajan deepened the canal but it silted up with sand from the desert. In the 7th century, the Arabian general Amr Ibn el-As had it dredged. After renewed silting, successively the Venetians and Napoleon planned its re-opening and improvement.

Today's canal was begun in 1859 by the French engineer Ferdinand de Lesseps and it was inaugurated 10 years later, November 16, 1869.

Cashing in on Osiris. Osiris was vitally important to the ancient Egyptian tourist trade. Worshippers would travel from afar to his santuary and spend good money when they got there. According to legend, this benign god of fertility was murdered by his brother, the desert-god Seth, and hurled in a box into the Nile. But the priests modified the story to the effect that Seth scattered parts of the body around the country. Abydos got the head, the Delta sanctuaries of Busiris and Mendes got the spine and phallus, while a leg ended up at Aswan on the island of Philae. Each piece bought a handsome part of the profits.

cinema and bazaar, where you will find a good selection of Bedouin jewellery, clothes and other craftwork. When you tire of watersports, play a round of golf on the 18-hole course designed by Gene Bates.

Hurghada

Founded only in the early 20th century, the town, 395 km (245 miles) south of Suez has, since the 1980s, seen an enormous boom in tourist development by American, European, Arab and Egyptian companies to make it the Red Sea coast's leading tourist resort. Beaches front 20 km (12 miles) of holiday villages and first-rate hotels, which provide excellent water sports facilities for windsurfing, sailing, deep-sea fishing, snorkelling and diving, and wonderful beaches of fine white sand. Safaris into the desert hinterland are organized by jeep or camel. The Aquarium at Ad-Dahar gives you a first glimpse of the tropical fish to be seen before going out to join them in the sea.

Hurghada's Islands

Take an excursion to Giftun Island for snorkelling and a fish barbecue or view its offshore lower depths in a submarine. Other islands—Shadwan, Shaab Abu Shiban, Umm Gammar, Abu Ramada, Shaab Abu Hashish and more—offer diving, snorkelling and fishing. Most but not all are ideal for family swimming and bathing. Enquire before signing on for the trip.

Safaga

Holiday villages are expanding the potential of what was originally just a commercial port with a small fishing harbour. There's a bonus in good seafood restaurants. The grand beaches and strong breezes are great for windsurfers, and the World Windsurfing Championships were held here in 1993.

Mons Claudianus

This popular excursion from Safaga leads you 50 km (30 miles) into the Red Mountains to an ancient Roman granite quarry and penal colony at the foot of Gebel Fatira. Emperor Hadrian had the quarry's black stone shipped to Rome for the portico in his Pantheon and for his country villa. Near the quarry are remains of an unfinished temple, a Roman camp, houses, workshops and stables.

El Quseir

Some 80 km (50 miles) south of Safaga, the old town is notable for the 16th-century fortress of Sultan Selim, its Bedouin street market and the modern resort area's beaches and coral reefs. In Pharaonic times, it was a major port and equipped the expedition of Queen Hatshepsut (1478–37) to the Land of Punt (coastal Ethiopia and Djibouti).

Marsa Alam

This is a small village, mostly inhabited by fishermen, with a charming little harbour and jetty. The Dokki Shooting Club organizes deep-sea fishing trips. Beside the more docile lobster and turtle, you may find yourself tackling shark or sharp-toothed moray eels lurking in the reefs. Diving facilities are being developed in the safer areas, with a nature reserve extending south all the way to Gebel Elba.

Berenice

The modern town is well known for its fishing and attracts Egyptian and foreign visitors to its health spas, secluded bays and coves for some great scuba diving. Watch for dolphins. The ancient city was founded in the 3rd century BC, named after the daughter of Ptolemy II Philadelphos. It prospered as a trading port for the Wadi Sakait emerald mines exploited in the interior from Pharaonic to Roman times. Near the modern town are remains of the Temples of Semiramis built by Roman emperors Trajan and Tiberius. The latter is depicted on an outer wall making sacrifices to the fertility god Min and, understandably, to the deity of the emerald mines.

Out to sea is the little island of **Zabargad**, mined for the semi-precious gem olivine from 1500 BC right up to the middle of the 20th century.

Bir Shalatein

This once major seaport on Egypt's border with Sudan is now used as a much appreciated diving area for charters organized from the more northerly resorts. Many like its secluded atmosphere, but special permits have to be booked in advance.

UNDERWATER WORLD

The Red Sea is host to over 800 fish species. The majority are harmless, but a few can be dangerous, like the stone-fish or the butterfly-fish and ominously named surgeon-fish. You can get stung by cassiopei jellyfish or nipped by crabs. Out in the deep are a few species of shark.

Photos: François Ender

1. Lion fish
2. Shoal of black-
   spotted grunts
   and bannerfish

3. Spiny lionfish
4. Masked butterfly fish
5. Red Sea grouper
6. Napoleon wrasse

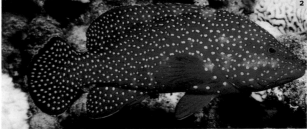

1. Parrot fish, surgeon fish and striped butterfly fish
2. Coral grouper
3. Blue-spotted stingray
4. Clown fish
5. Striped butterfly fish
6. Giant clam

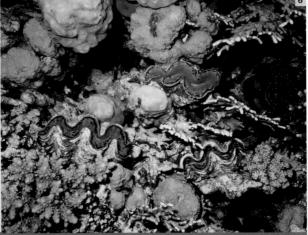

The rising sun sets alight the peaks of Mount Sinai, where Moses received the Ten Commandments.

Huber/Olimpio

Sinai

The peninsula that has served both as bridge and barrier between Egypt and Israel now peacefully combines Biblical legend and history with delightful beach resorts. Inland from the coast, the desert is for the most part a dramatic landscape of multicoloured craggy mountains with a rare oasis in its valleys.

The beach resorts are at the southern tip of the peninsula and on the east coast facing the Gulf of Aqaba. Ancient sites, including those pinpointed by tradition as landmarks of the Hebrews' Exodus from Egypt, are dotted along the west coast south of the Suez Canal. Mount Sinai itself and St Catherine's Monastery can be reached on an excursion from the resorts.

West Coast

An hour's drive south of the Suez Canal are the Springs of Moses, **Uyun Musa**, believed to be a miraculous creation of the Israelites' leader. It is now a tiny palm-shaded pool tended by Bedouins selling souvenirs. Hot springs on the beach some 80 km (50 miles) further south are identified as **Hammam Pharaun**, the Pharaoh's Baths. Inland from the oil wells of Abu Rudeis are the ancient turquoise mines of **Wadi Maghara**, another stopping place of the Hebrews on their way to Mount Sinai. Nearby, at **Serabit El Khadim**, are remains of the rock-cut Temple of Hathor.

Sharm El Sheikh

The sports and leisure facilities here match the quality of the superb fine sandy beaches. The resort's position at the southern tip of the Sinai peninsula makes it a dream location for snorkelling and scuba diving—with expert on-the-spot training for beginners. Glass-bottom boats let non-swimmers share in some of the fun. The junction of the shallow Gulf of Suez and awesomely deep Gulf of Aqaba brings to Sharm an unrivalled collection of easily accessible corals and exotic fish. Visit, too, the nearby marine nature reserve of Ras Mohammed, where even waders in the shallows can spot wonderful fish. Respect the iron law: "Look, but do not touch."

The Sinai mountains provide a grand backdrop to the beaches and stellar attraction is a sunset safari into the foothills for a romantic supper served up by the local Bedouin.

East Coast

The resorts north of Sharm El Sheikh have grown out of the infrastructure left at coastal villages during the Israeli occupation of the Sinai.

The Bedouins. The romantic image of the desert nomads has been dented by contact with the modern world. These days, camels in the Sinai tend to be reserved for taking tourists for a ride. With asphalt roads across the desert and petrol more plentiful than water, many Bedouins have traded in their dromedary for a Toyota truck. Not without regrets: when these new ships of the desert break down far from civilization, the driver can't barbecue the carburettor until he is rescued.

istockphoto.com/Podgoresk

Dahab
What was once a sleepy fishing port is blossoming into a well-equipped beach resort offering first-rate facilities for snorkelling, deep-sea diving, fishing and just lazing on a beach mattress.

Nuweiba
Besides expanding its tourist amenities, the village is noted for its good fish restaurants with the rare phenomenon of menus in both Hebrew and Arabic, as well as English.

Inland, to the north, the **Coloured Canyon** takes its name from the multi-coloured layers of its walls, reached through a narrow slit. Excursions are organized by many hotels.

Taba
On the Israeli border, the resort has the most modern of luxury hotels and also beach bungalows, ready to link up with Eilat and Aqaba on the new Riviera. South of town, out in the bay, is Pharoah's Island where you can visit Sultan Saladin's 12th-century fortress. The desert-type 18-hole championship golf course at Taba Heights, designed by John Sanford, looks over three countries.

Mount Sinai
According to tradition, it is Gebel Musa (Mount Moses) on which the Ten Commandments were given to the Israelites. It attracts thousands of pilgrims each year for the pre-dawn climb. Steps have been cut in the rocky path to the summit 2,285 m (7,494 ft) above sea level. Start early—the view at sunrise over the gold and purple mountain peaks will convince you that a god must be hanging around here somewhere.

St Catherine's Monastery
The Greek Orthodox monastery at the foot of Mount Sinai is said to stand on the site where Moses

encountered the Burning Bush. The monastery church of the Alexandrian saint, whose remains were found on nearby Mount Catherine, has a remarkable collection of Byzantine icons. But its most cherished artworks are the 6th-century mosaics in the ceiling of the apse at the rear of the church. Take a stroll in the monastery garden. Or contemplate in the Ossuary the skulls and bones of hundreds of long-gone monks and one archbishop with his skeleton still in one piece and clothed in his monastic robes.

Wadi Faran

The road west of St Catherine's takes you back into Biblical history, retracing the Hebrews' path from the Red Sea to Mount Sinai. Coming from St Catherine's, look out for a signposted mound on the east side of the road known as the Shrine of Aaron, where the brother of Moses is believed to have erected the Golden Calf. Further down the road is the Plain of Raha, the Hebrews' encampment. From here, the road turns north through a craggy landscape to the Wadi Faran oasis.

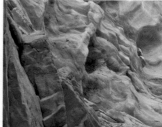

Protected by a wall, St Catherine's Monastery at the foot of Mt Sinai. | The Coloured Canyon near Dahab. | An idyllic beach, sandwiched between mountains and sea.

Alexandria's architecture shows
Mediterranean and Oriental influences.

hemis.fr/Orne

Alexandria and the Mediterranean Coast

Cultural capital of the ancient Greco-Roman Mediterranean, Egypt's second city has lost its historical grandeur, but the spirit of the people is still proudly independent. This is a relaxed, outward-looking gateway to Europe and western Asia, with a gentle climate that attracts prosperous Cairotes for their summer vacations. Resorts popular with Egyptians are blossoming along the Mediterranean coast to the Libyan frontier.

Alexandria

True to Alexander the Great's intentions when he founded the city in 332 BC, Alexandria is still Egypt's main seaport. Two deep-water harbours serve commercial, fishing and cruise traffic. With a population of 4.5 million, it is the distribution centre for fisheries and cotton manufacture. More important for gourmets, the city has the best seafood restaurants in the country.

The Seafront

The broad curve of the Corniche promenade begins at the ancient eastern harbour. On the edge of the harbour promontory, the fortress of Sultan Qaitbay, now housing a naval museum, stands on the site of the ancient Pharos lighthouse. Built by the Ptolemies in the 3rd century BC, the beacon, 120 m (393 ft) high, rated with the Giza pyramids as one of the Seven Wonders of the World until toppled by earthquakes. On the west side of the promontory is the flamboyant Ras El Tin palace, in which King Farouk signed his abdication.

Bibliotheca Alexandrina

The Ptolemies' Great Library, founded in 288 BC and famous throughout the Mediterranean world for its 490,000 scrolls, disappeared in the fires of Alexandria's invaders, its treasures lost forever. But a new UNESCO-sponsored Bibliotheca Alexandrina has been created on the northeast side of town. The elegant Norwegian-designed building has sweeping marble walls etched with alphabets both ancient and modern. It includes conference facilities, a planetarium, two museums and an art gallery.

The Ancient City

The few monuments of the Greco-Roman past stand in fascinating juxtaposition with the modern town. The Roman baths and a theatre of the 3rd century are tucked away among tenements of the Kom el-Dikka neighbourhood. In the Catacombs at Kom el-Shuqafa, alongside tombs recalling pharaonic motifs is a hall where Roman soldiers were buried with their horses.

Many of Alexandria's old trams once ran through the streets of Copenhagen.

Beside a sphinx overlooking high-rise apartment blocks, the pink granite Pompey's Pillar with its ornate Corinthian capital is a monument not to the Roman general but to Emperor Diocletian, around AD 300, erected on the site of a Ptolemaic temple.

Greco-Roman Museum
The museum, founded in 1893, includes sculptures of Alexander the Great, Julius Caesar and Emperor Hadrian, and a rare medallion-portrait of Cleopatra.

There is also a collection of sculpture and other finds from the pharaonic era in the Delta and Nile Valley, including statues of Ramses II and the goddess Isis. The museum is closed for several years, for renovation.

Alexandria National Museum
Housed in an Italianate palace, it exhibits relics of the age of the pharaohs on the first floor, Greco-Roman finds on the second, and Coptic, Islamic and modern pieces on the third. Mummies are displayed in the basement.

Latterday Alexandria
The town's Islamic buildings are mostly of recent construction. The **Mosque of Abu El Abbas**, built in 1769, was restored in the 1940s. The graceful minarets and domes honouring the 13th-century Islamic scholar can be seen looming above the Corniche.

For a glimpse of the opulent life of King Farouk and his family, visit the **Jewellery Museum** housed in a palatial mansion in the sedate Zizinia quarter. Apart from the diamonds and rubies, the bathroom fixtures alone were worth several years' salary of the plumbers who installed them.

Montazah Palace
On the east side of town, the 19th-century summer residence of Mohammed Ali's playboy

descendants is an extravagant combination of Italian Gothic and Turkish Ottoman. Walk through the delightful public gardens of orange trees and umbrella pines down to the harbour and watch the local fishermen.

The Beaches
Alexandria has sandy beaches right downtown, just beyond the harbours. Others popular for swimming are Agami to the west and Maamoura and Aboukir, east of Montazah. **Aboukir** won its place in the history books for Admiral Nelson's devastating victory over Napoleon in 1798. Today, the town is run down but gourmets appreciate its great seafood restaurant.

Wadi Natrun
South of Alexandria, in the desert near the delta, this "valley", in fact a flat area surrounded by lakes, is known for its four Coptic monasteries, all that have survived since medieval times when this was a great Christian community. It was founded by St Macarius the Great who retreated here in 330. In the 4th century Anchorites dwelled in caves and began building monasteries. The area became the official residence of the Coptic patriarch. Each monastery is protected by a high fortified wall, around churches, living quarters and a keep.

El Alamein
A pilgrimage 100 km (60 miles) west along the coast from Alexandria takes you back to a landmark of 20th-century history, the battlefield that turned the tide of Germany's North African campaign in World War II. A museum with tanks, cannons and other relics commemorates the brutal confrontation between Rommel's German and Italian forces and the Allied and British Commonwealth troops under Montgomery. The war dead of the opposing armies are honoured in cemeteries nearby. Be careful not to wander too far off the highway as the desert still conceals scores of unexploded shells and landmines.

Sidi Abdel Rahman
Within easy reach of El Alamein, this resort commands miles of unspoiled sandy beaches. There are good opportunities here for windsurfing and deep-sea fishing with a hired boat.

Marsa Matruh
This other theatre of World War II operations is now a blissfully peaceful fishing port and capital of Egypt's western Mediterranean region. It is a fast-growing resort with fine beaches, modest hotels and holiday homes, all offering good facilities and equipment for water sports.

An island of green in the midst of the sands: Dakhla in the Libyan Desert.

Western Oases

The exotic oases of the Western Desert offer one of Egypt's most exciting tours—by definition well off the beaten track and well worth the effort. Travelling northwest from Luxor, the desert route leaves the Nile at Assiut, striking out across more than 1,000 km of dunes and steep escarpments of golden sand to the oases of lush palm groves, orchards and pools of cool spring water amid remains of ancient citadels and temples.

The tour traces a crescent from El Kharga via Dakhla north to Farafra and across the ghostly landscape of the White Desert up to Bahariya and the Valley of the Golden Mummies. For those continuing on from Bahariya, the route takes off at a tangent west to the grand oasis of Siwa out near the Libyan frontier where Alexander the Great is believed to have consulted its legendary oracle.

The oases have been settled since prehistoric times, but while Siwa remained in splendid isolation until the 19th century, Egypt's ancient rulers took an active interest in the other "inner" oases. They were valued both for their agricultural riches—olives, dates and other fruit—and for their strategic positions as garrisons to resist outside invaders. Besides the pharaohs, the oases have been ruled by Persians, Greeks, Romans, Mamelukes, Turks and the British. Today, new roads and all-terrain vehicles have opened them up to larger settlement and a burgeoning tourist traffic. To accommodate Nile-dwellers displaced by the Aswan Dam's creation of Lake Nasser, the three southerly oases —Kharga, Dakhla and Farafra— have been grouped in the New Valley Governorate with Kharga as its capital.

Kharga Oasis

For the new status of this oasis as a regional capital, with a population of 60,000, a modern town of multi-storey hotels, residential and office buildings has sprung up at the town of El Kharga, most of them along Sharia Gamal Abdel Nasser, the main street. On the main square stands a modern allegorical sculpture of Mother Egypt and her children—the oases. Shoppers may like to visit El Kharga's carpet and pottery factories.

Museum of Antiquities

The museum exhibits findings from the region's archaeological sites, notably death masks and painted sarcophagi from the Greco-Roman era; mummified eagles, ibises and rams from the tombs of El Muzawaka and artefacts from the tombs of 6th-

Dynasty Balat governors, both at Dakhla; Coptic pottery and textiles and decorative friezes from the 12th-century Fatimids and the Ottoman era.

Old Town

The town's more romantic, older quarter of orange and blue coloured mud-brick houses is clustered around Midan Showla. At its heart is a bustling bazaar, near the narrow winding Darb El Sindadiyya, an ancient street roofed with palm tree trunks dating in part back to the 10th century. In among the old dwellings are passageways serving as storage barns and stables.

Around El Kharga

North of town, the **Temple of Hibis** (6th century BC), one of the rare monuments built by the Persians in Egypt, has a fine decor of painted vultures and reliefs depicting the emperor Darius welcoming Egyptian deities.

The **Bagawat Necropolis** comprises more than 250 mud-brick chapels, many of them decorated with Coptic murals—including the Exodus Chapel showing

Rocks sculpted by erosion in the White Desert. | Mosque fresco on a mud-brick home at Farafra Oasis. | Farmers returning home from the fields near Bawiti, Bahariya Oasis.

Moses leading the Jews of Egypt with the pharaoh's army in hot pursuit and the Peace Chapel depicting Adam and Eve and Noah's Ark.

South of town, the **Bulaq hot springs** are reputedly good for relieving rheumatism and skin ailments. The **Baris oasis**, with its modern Nubian-style houses, has been abandoned because, to their intended residents, they looked like tombs.

Dakhla Oasis

Some 200 km (124 miles) north-west of Kharga, the greenery of Dakhla nestles against a soaring backdrop of rose-hued cliffs. With a population of 75,000, the oasis covers 420 sq km (168 sq miles), including over 12,000 ha (30,000 acres) of cultivated land tended by 14 farming communities. Forever fending off the invasion of sand dunes, its fields and orchards boast fig trees, date palms, mulberry trees and groves of orange and lemon. In prehistoric times, the region's great lake dried up and many of the inhabitants moved east to settle in the Nile Valley. Today, new settlers combine modern technology with the time-honoured irrigation methods of water wheels of palm timber driven by buffaloes and distributing the water in *saqiya* clay jars. The water is drawn from Dakhla's 520 wells.

Mut

Presenting the modern face of Dakhla, the medieval capital of the oasis is named after the ancient Egyptian mother goddess who, together with her husband Amun and son Khons, made up the Theban Triad. A complex of offices, banks and apartment buildings extends away from the citadel and labyrinthine old town of narrow alleys lined with mud-brick houses with carved lintels. These are slowly being abandoned in favour of standard concrete apartments.

The small Inheritance Museum is housed in a typical old dwelling and displays various elements of oasis life.

El Qasr

Built on a Roman settlement north of Mut, this town is well worth visiting for its warren of twisting covered streets of pink or russet-coloured mud-brick houses. Notice the doorways' intricately carved wooden lintels. The town has a 12th-century Ayyubid mosque with medieval Koranic inscriptions on its lintels and an even older *madrassa* (religious school) with a splendid rooftop view over the town.

Just west of town, the Theban Triad are celebrated at the temple of **Deir El Hagar**, with hot sulphur springs and the ancient tombs of **El Muzawaka** nearby.

Farafra Oasis

Tucked away 310 km (192 miles) north of Dakhla, the most modest of the oases was known in pharaonic times as Ta-iht, Land of the Cows. Direct descendants of those cows (depicted on ancient tomb-friezes on the Nile) still roam around the oasis pastures—and are often smuggled out on back roads to Bahariya. Watered by cool streams and rivulets, Farafra's orchards provide apricots, figs, dates, guavas and olives. A dozen modern hamlets have been added to the oasis' one town, Qasr El Farafra. Its population of 4,000 mainly Bedouin live in mud-brick houses. Most are painted blue to ward off the "evil eye", some decorated with friezes of birds, animals and desert landscapes. Known for their Muslim piety, Farafrans are said to have lost track of the calendar and had to send a rider to Dakhla to be sure of holding Friday prayers on the right day.

White Desert

North of Farafra on the road to Bahariya, a desert floor of hard white chalk stretches out in a depression of eerie canyons dotted with bizarre monoliths. These wind-eroded "sculptures" take the form of camels, donkeys, desert nomads, trees, giant mushrooms, some of them as high as two-storey houses. The best time to visit is after the heat of the day

Corbis/Watts

Mud-brick constructions at Bahariya cemetery.

on a starlit or moonlit night and ponder a moment that Egypt's Persian conqueror King Cambyses is believed to lost an army of 50,000 men here around 600 BC.

Bahariya Oasis

Beyond the White Desert on the route back to Cairo, the oasis is located in a depression of golden sands some 90 km (56 miles) long and 40 km (25 miles) wide surrounded by a ring of black basalt hills. The town of **Bawiti** is built along a ridge overlooking groves of date palms and olives, apricot orchards and fields of rice, corn and vegetables. (In pre-Muslim days, the oasis exported wine to the Nile Valley.) Supplementing the houses' mud bricks is masonry from pharaonic temples and a Roman arch of triumph. The Oasis Heritage Museum exhibits works of a local sculptor.

Valley of the Golden Mummies

Discovered in 1996 and made public three years later, the 2,000-year-old necropolis 6 km (4 miles) south of Bawiti is believed to contain thousands of mummified men, women and children from the Greco-Roman era. The mummies are of four kinds. Some of them have gilded face masks and ornate chest-plates (hence the valley's name), others were wrapped in linen or buried in brightly painted *cartonnage*

coffins, and some were entombed in simple ceramic anthropomorphic coffins. During an excavation programme that is expected to last 50 years, public access is limited. Ten mummies can be seen in the modern museum, some have splendid masks.

Siwa Oasis

On the outer limits of the Western Desert's Great Sand Sea at the Libyan border, Siwa is very much a world apart, even from the other oases. Its 23,000 mainly Berber inhabitants speak their own Siwi dialect, not Arabic, and generally observe much stricter traditional dress and decorous behaviour than elsewhere in Egypt. Siwa's dates and olives have been famous for centuries, and the sweet waters of its 1000 springs much prized for their medicinal properties. Siwa town combines concrete housing with older mudbrick dwellings around a central market.

To the east, near the village of **Aghurmi**, restored ruins of the Temple of Amun (6th century BC) mark the site of the Siwan Oracle consulted by Alexander the Great in 331 BC. To seal his divine right to rule Egypt, he needed the Oracle's confirmation that he was a descendant of Zeus (Greece's equivalent of Amun). Whatever he was told has remained a secret to this day.

Copts

Coptic Christians trace their origins back to the evangelism of St Mark in Alexandria in the 1st century. Their language, used only in the liturgy, was originally a dialect of ancient Egyptian. They founded Christianity's monastic tradition, seeking refuge in the desert as much from fear of persecution as a desire for meditation. Today, they number some 8 per cent of the population and are prominent in business and industry. Their most famous son is Boutros Ghali, former UN Secretary General. Though bearing the title of Patriarch of Alexandria, the church leader is now based in Cairo. Complicated doctrinal conflicts have kept them separate from the Eastern Orthodox Church, but much of their art and church architecture is Byzantine in inspiration. On the other hand, they practise circumcision and observe similar dietary laws to those of their Muslim and Jewish neighbours.

Islam

The name means in Arabic "submission to" Allah. Islam's book, the Koran, covers all features of everyday life, in and outside the mosque—marriage, property, work, eating, drinking and sleeping, as well as prayer. The Koran is Mohammed's presentation of Allah's message as he received it from the angel Gabriel. The Allah of the Koran is a loving, just and merciful God. His will determines the lives of all men and women. Their actions on earth determine their place in heaven or hell. The inspired merchant of Mecca (570–632) honoured the Jewish patriarchs and Jesus as pious but fallible prophets. As the last prophet, he had the last word. It was carried to Egypt in 641, nine years after the death of Mohammed.

Mummies

The most ancient mummies are up to 5,000 years old, but now scarcely more than hair, skin and bone remain, conserved by the desert climate. Techniques to preserve the body for eternity developed progressively over the centuries, reaching a peak of refinement by the time of Tutankhamun and Ramses II. The whole process took 70 days—40 to dry out the body,

15 for embalming and 15 for bandaging. The embalmers first removed all internal organs (except the heart, kept as the seat of understanding) for separate storage. For a natural look, the dehydrated body was coated in oils and resin to keep it supple and padded with mud, sawdust and linen. Head, fingers, toes, arms and legs were wrapped separately to preserve the body's contours. Less care was taken when mummifying animals.

Painting and Sculpture

Ancient Egypt's artistic conventions are quite different from those of European art. Human figures on murals and carved reliefs often adopt an impossibly distorted pose. The head is seen in profile but the eye is shown in full, shoulders fully frontal but torso three-quarters, then striding legs from the side. The artist ignores realism to present each feature of the body to its best advantage. While a muscular torso was an obvious sculptural symbol of youth, a scribe's wrinkled belly portrayed his wisdom, not his senility. Pharaohs grabbing enemies by the hair and thwacking them with a cudgel in most cases never went near a battlefield, but their dominance of foreigners had to be shown. Scenes of sacrificial offerings show their special relationship with the gods, who may then offer the supreme seal of familiarity by kissing the king. These ritual sterotypes contrast with the striking reality in scenes of everyday life of farmers, butchers and bakers. Realism is carried to extravagant lengths under maverick pharaoh Akhenaton, happily portrayed with thick lips, pot-belly and bloated thighs.

Papyrus

Papyrus paper was made from a plant *(Cyperus papyrus)* growing profusely in the Delta marsh-lands which died out in the Roman era. It was a versatile material, also used for making boats, ropes and baskets. The plant has since been re-imported from Sudan and grown again for use in the tourist industry. To make this first buff-coloured form of paper, the fibrous pith of the papyrus plant's stem was cut into strips. These were soaked then laid out side by side to be superimposed in two crisscrossing layers and beaten together, with the pith's sap glueing them into one smooth sheet.

Kanafa pastries made from thin strands of dough, similar to shredded wheat.

DINING OUT

Egyptian cuisine is a combination of the good things that the fertile Nile Valley and Delta have been providing since the time of the pharaohs, and the influence of Arabic and more emphatically Turkish cooking. One of the surprises is to see many of the same dishes that the pharaohs enjoyed at banquets depicted on 3,000-year-old friezes in their tombs: pigeon, quail and duck, crushed wheat and vegetables, figs, dates and apricots.

For variety, foreign restaurants are also available in abundance. These range from the nondescript fare known as "international" or more mystifyingly "continental" to quite good Italian, Indian, Chinese and Japanese. But on the whole, beware of claims to serve French cuisine, too often in pompous, flashy settings with little or no authenticity.

In addition, there are other Arabic restaurants, Lebanese or Moroccan, serving refined variations on Egyptian cuisine.

To Start With...

Many newcomers never get further than the wonderful menu of Egyptian starters. Known as *mezzeh,* these are different kinds of savoury salads and yoghurt, concoctions of puréed and garlicky sesame, chickpeas and beans *(ful)*, and minced meatballs or fish-paste. It is best to eat them with torn-off pieces of traditional floppy *pita*-style bread *(aysh)*. For two or more diners, it is fun to order an assortment. But pace yourself if you want to handle a main dish of meat or fish later. Here are some favourite *mezzeh*: *taamiah* or *falaafil*, deep-fried balls of bean or chickpea paste, herbs and spices; *makhallal*, spicy pickled vegetables, often also served as an accompanying condiment to a main dish; *tahina*, a tangy purée of sesame seed; *subeit*, cold cuttlefish (or squid) salad; *megdra*, lentils and rice; *baba ganoug*, tahina mixed with eggplant (aubergine).

If you want to restrict yourself to just one starter, try the famous *molokhia,* a vegetable soup of dark greens served with rice.

Fish and Seafood

Since ancient times, fish and seafood have been an important part of the Egyptian diet. Today, bumptious Alexandria claims the best seafood from its Mediterranean waters — giant prawns, red mullet, sea bass and bream — grilled or pan-fried with an occasional touch of cumin spice. The Red Sea and Sinai resorts are more than honourable rivals with a wide range of fish, plus good shrimp, squid, crab and spiny lobster (*langouste*). A supreme delicacy is a barbecued *kebab* of monkfish.

Meat Dishes

Lamb or more often mutton is most popular served as *kebab* in marinated pieces, *kofta,* minced, or chops, all grilled or barbecued on the skewer. *Shwarma* is the Egyptian lamb equivalent of the Turkish *döner kebab,* roasted layers of meat wrapped around a vertical spit. Quail and pigeon from the Delta are stuffed, or spreadeagled and grilled to be eaten whole (the pigeons may still have their heads on). Meat is generally accompanied by rice (*ruzz*) or bread. The rice may be mixed wih nuts, onions, vegetables or small pieces of meat.

Desserts

Egypt benefits from the wealth of fresh fruit both from the Delta and the oases of the Western Desert: bananas, figs, apricots, oranges, guavas, and of course dates that you never imagined existed in such variety — red, yellow, black, brown, sweet and bittersweet. *Om-ali* is a delicious national delicacy, baked rice in milk with almonds, pistachios and raisins. *Mahallabiyah* is a smoother, less sweet version. But forget all calorie counts if you're going for the honey-laced pastries: flaky *baklava* with nuts, *atayeef* filled with cheese or honey or both; and cubes of *loukoum* — Turkish delight.

Soft Drinks

The great saviour on your desert excursions is the mineral water bottled from local springs. Bottles neatly named Baraka ("good luck") are available everywhere.

All the international brands of soft drinks are sold, good fruit juices and the local dark red hibiscus drink, *karkadeh*, served ice-cold. It is best to order your drinks without ice; it's not worth risking a stomach upset.

Beer and Wine

Alcohol is taboo for Muslims, but the Copts (and more easy-going Muslims) keep the beer and wine industry going. Besides the many foreign brands of beer, the popular local brew is the light Stella lager. Some prefer the more expensive Stella export.

Connoisseurs should not expect too much of the wines of the Delta's vineyards. The whites, with names like Cleopatra or Nefertiti, are better than the reds, of which Château Gianaclis and Omar Khayyam are the most acceptable. Rubis d'Egypte is the local rosé. European wines are available in luxury hotels but are very, very expensive.

The adventurous may like to try *zibib*, the Egyptian equivalent of the Mediterranean anise-flavoured pastis, made here from a distillation of grapes or, yes, dates.

hemis.fr/Frumm

Bernard Joliat

Herbs and spices in the bazaar. | **Techniques in preparing bread in ancient ovens of baked mud have not changed since the days of the pharaohs.**

Even if you don't smoke, a hubble-bubble pipe can make a nice ornament!

SHOPPING

Buying a souvenir of your stay in Egypt should always be a pleasurable pastime. When buying a necklace in Cairo or a statue in Luxor, even if you don't like bargaining, go through the motions. Like the coffee or mint tea offered you at the counter, it's part of the game.

Where?

If possible, plan to shop during the last part of your trip so that you don't have to carry stuff around too long. Ideally, with a day or two in Cairo at the end of your stay, you can buy most of your presents at the Khan El Khalili bazaar. The Egyptian Museum's shops offer the broadest range of books and souvenirs of ancient Egypt, but at fixed prices. At Luxor, you'll find the best bargains in good-quality copies of ancient statues are in the artisans' workshops over on the west bank rather than in Luxor's tourist bazaar. Aswan is best for spices and perfumes. Hurghada has a good bazaar for Bedouin products. Nostalgics will like Alexandria's antique-cum-junk shops for bizarre Oriental Victorian paraphernalia.

What?

The best buys are those that capture the atmosphere of Egypt—a jewel, perfume, garment, papyrus painting or small sculpture—another good reason not to start shopping before you've gained a feeling for the place.

On the purely practical side, make sure your purchases are not too big or too fragile to pack. Old hands at this game always carry an extra collapsible bag in their luggage.

Amber

From pale yellow to rich brandy brown, this is the prized material of traditional Egyptian worrybeads or cigarette-holders for men and jewellery for women. Alas, the best amber is not cheap and the second-best is often not amber.

Antiques

You are not allowed to export authentic antiquities without a government licence, and you won't get one. It may be a consolation to know that authentic antiquities are just not available on the open market anyway. Do not be taken in by those men who surreptitiously pull out from the folds of their djellaba "artefacts" wrapped in old newspaper in the Valley of the Kings.

Bedouin Folk Art
Around the Sinai and Red Sea resorts, you'll find embroidered robes and hats and brightly coloured necklaces and bracelets.

Brass and Copperware
This is a speciality of Khan El Khalili, where you can watch your samovar, tray or Turkish-coffee set being made in one of the many workshops.

Clothes
Light Egyptian cotton is among the finest in the world, great for T-shirts. The traditional voluminous collarless *gallabiya* makes a comfortable beach robe or housecoat, particularly good for camouflaging the belly. Modern Egyptian fashions for ladies can be attractive.

The burgundy felt fez or tarbush is disdained by Egyptians as a relic of the colonial age and may not last back home longer than a one-time party joke.

Cosmetics and Perfumes
Egyptian henna and kohl are much admired by people who know about such things. They also highly recommend perfumes not pretending to be anything but very good imitations of top French brands.

Games
Boardgames for chess, dominoes and backgammon are available in alabaster, ebony and mother of pearl.

Jewellery
Among precious or semi-precious stones at Khan El Khalili, you'll find bargains in lapis lazuli, topaz and amethyst. Craftsmanship in gold and silverware is very good, if less sophisticated than in Europe. Look for pieces modelled on the treasures of King Tutankhamun or intricate Islamic designs. Hieroglyphic cartouches are popular as earrings and pendants engraved with the name of your choice. Usually they will be delivered directly to your hotel or cruise ship.

Leather Goods
The bags are robust rather than handsome, and the sewing tends to be at best rustic.

Papyrus
Before buying, watch the ancient technique of papyrus-making in workshops near the Giza pyramids and at Cairo's Papyrus Institute on a downtown river-

boat. Themes from ancient temple friezes and the hieroglyphic alphabet are attractively hand-painted on papyrus wall-hangings, calendars, bookmarks.

Sculpture
Copies of the ancient statues—pharaohs, scribes, sacred baboons and cat-goddesses—vary in quality from crude mass-produced work in soapstone and synthetics to meticulously crafted pieces in alabaster, black granite or olive-hued basalt. (If you're told it's granite and your fingernail leaves a mark, it's soapstone.)

Water Pipes
These splendid smoking instruments can be a killer to the unsuspecting throat but make fine ornaments. They are variously known as *narguileh, shisha,* hubble-bubble or hookah—as smoked by Alice's Caterpillar.

Wood Carvings
The craftmanship that goes into the traditional lattice screens, *mashrabiya,* is used on a smaller scale for more portable boxes or trays of sandalwood or cedar inlaid with mother of pearl.

Typical Egyptian crafts: inlaid mother-of-pearl; beaten metalwork; brass lamps; colourful wall-hangings woven by Bedouins.

istockphoto.com/Awad

hemis.fr/Orteo

Huber/Schmid

istockphoto.com/Kudinov

Conditions are great for windsurfing, here in the Red Sea near Hurghada.

SPORTS

Even if a beach resort is not on your itinerary, a pool is never far away for you to escape the heat and freshen up with a few lengths or harmless paddling. Plan any more strenuous sport for early morning or after the heat of the day. You may also find a health club adjoining the swimming pool for a work-out and massage.

On Land...

Many of the major hotels offer court facilities for tennis and squash, including lessons with tennis professionals, but you should take your own racket.

Cairo and Alexandria have private 18-hole golf courses. Your hotel can get you temporary membership in Cairo's otherwise exclusive clubs on Gezireh Island.

Horses, camels and mules can be hired for riding to the desert monuments or going off into the dunes for an overnight safari accompanied by Bedouin guides.

At Luxor, you can rent a bicycle in town, take it across on the ferry to tour the Valley of the Kings or even put it on a train to visit towns up- and downriver.

On Water...

The Nile is a beautiful river, but don't even think of swimming in it. Stick to the hotel or cruise-boat pool or wait till you get to the sea. The Mediterranean provides a great breeze for windsurfers, and snorkelling and scuba diving are big at the Red Sea and Sinai resorts. Both Sharm El Sheikh and Hurghada provide modern diving equipment and expert training for deep-sea novices, and the underwater life is simply amazing.

You can charter boats for deep-sea fishing at all the resorts and get the hotel-chef to barbecue the catch.

... and Indoors

For some, all the sport they need is the wristwork of rolling dice or stretching the biceps to place a chip at the roulette table. Casinos are found only in the tourists' hotels as they are forbidden to Muslims. In Cairo, Alexandria or Ismailiya, the sign "Casino" refers to places of entertainment without gambling.

The colossal statue of Ramses II at Abu Simbel is one of the most impressive of Egyptian monuments.

ART AND ARCHITECTURE

Before you arrive, the poster image of Egypt presents art as super-human in every way: the massive pyramids of Giza, the gigantic temples of Luxor and Karnak, the colossal statues of Ramses II and his queen at Abu Simbel. Once in Egypt, you discover that the pharaohs' artists also have a keen sense of the human dimension in ordinary life. Particularly in the tomb frescoes, they like to show people and their domestic animals, the birds they hunt, the fish they eat and the cereals they grow for their bread.

Each image has a religious or magic symbolic meaning that the ancient Egyptians carried with them into the next world. And the aridity of the desert has preserved this art for the eternity inscribed in the *Book of the Dead*, as the birthright of every Egyptian.

Pyramids

The pyramids containing the tombs of the pharaoh and his family began as gigantic versions of the large tombs known as *mastaba* built for royalty and nobles alike. (*Mastaba* means "bench" in Arabic, though the slab seems closer in shape to a massive gold ingot.) The first, so-called Step Pyramid built by architect Imhotep at Saqqara for the pharaoh Djoser around 2670

BC, started out as three superimposed *mastaba*-like platforms which were then extended and raised to form a pyramid of six tiers or steps.

Nearly a century later, the sheer-faced pyramids of Giza were built around a similar central core of stepped mastaba slabs, using rough limestone, and then smoothed off with a finer limestone casing. This can still be seen at the base of Kheops' Great Pyramid and more clearly at the apex of the second biggest pyramid, built for Khephren.

In the absence of sufficiently sturdy wheeled carts (or a pulley system for hoisting yet to be invented), the Great Pyramid's 2 million huge 2.5-ton blocks were in all likelihood tugged along mudbrick ramps on sledge-like rockers. Inside, to relieve the pyramid's weight bearing down on the royal burial chambers, empty compartments were added as structural supports. Typically, corridors lead up from ground level through a grand gallery to the King's burial chamber, with side corridors across to the Queen's and down to a chamber below ground level for other family members. Many of the monuments seem uncomplicated in their basic architecture (see below). In fact the simplicity conceals a whole world of intricate design.

Fig. 1: Pyramid of Kheops.

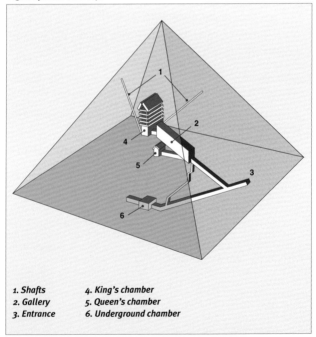

1. *Shafts*	4. *King's chamber*
2. *Gallery*	5. *Queen's chamber*
3. *Entrance*	6. *Underground chamber*

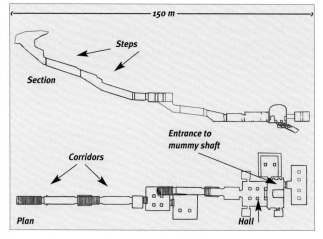

Fig. 2: Section and plan of a typical tomb in the Valley of Kings.

Tombs in Valley of the Kings

After the Old Kingdom, economic necessity forced the pharaohs to abandon the exorbitant costs of the pyramids for Thebes' more modest—but still opulent—subterranean tombs on the west bank of the Nile in the Valley of the Kings. Inconspicuous doorways hewn from the granite escarpment made them less easy prey for the grave-robbers than those ostentatious piles at Saqqara and Giza.

Since life after death for the Egyptians was conceived as continuing without much change,

their tombs were designed "just like home" and in the case of royalty or the nobles, like a palace. Each was furnished with the deceased's daily needs and offerings for the gods. For a pharaoh like Tutankhamun, besides the sumptuously decorated burial chamber with a sarcophagus laden with bejewelled regalia, the tomb had a chapel for worship and other rooms for food, treasure, clothes, weapons, kitchen utensils, farm implements and other commodities of everyday life. Stairways and long, deep corridors connect the rooms and chapel, leading at the lowest level to the burial chamber itself. The goods for the afterlife were furnished both in actual and symbolic form, painted in frescoed friezes or carved in bas-relief, the grandeur of this decoration being an artistic tribute to the gods as precious as the treasures themselves.

Temples at Karnak and Luxor

Ancient Egyptian temples may be divided into two types. Cult temples, the house of the gods, provided for the community to worship in prayer halls, and incorporated housing for priests. Mortuary or funerary temples were shrines for the more specific cult of a dead pharaoh, built near his tomb and linking his image to that of one or more guardian deities. At Thebes, the cult temples were erected at Karnak and Luxor, while the mortuary temples were over in the Theban Necropolis.

The act of worship in a cult temple constitutes a cosmic journey in which the earth is the sanctuary's causeways and the temple floor, while the heaven is the star-studded ceilings. Inexorably, as the floor slopes upward and the ceilings grow progressively lower, the worshipper is brought face to face with the temple's chief deity in the innermost sanctuary, the Other World.

A ceremonial causeway bordered by statues, generally an avenue of sphinxes, leads from a quay at the Nile to the temple's monumental entrance between two towering pylons. In an open courtyard, colossal statues of the pharaoh and obelisks flank the path to a first great columned basilica known as the hypostyle hall, then perhaps another. Each is decorated with sculptures and friezes that honour king and god alike. Beyond the halls is a votive chamber for offerings to the deities and then the holy of holies, the gods' innermost sanctuary. On either side are the temple's treasure chambers and storage rooms for cult objects.

Outside the temple, but still within its precincts, is a sacred lake providing water for rituals, together with the priests' dormitories, kitchens and other living quarters.

Designs for the pharaohs' mortuary temples presented a similar concept of cosmic journey, though this time they went from the land of the living to the land of the Afterlife. Set inland from the Nile's west bank, the magnificent temple of Queen Hatshepsut takes her worshippers up ramps linking three colonnaded terraces to a hypostyle hall and the inner sanctuary, the whole carved from the hillside's limestone rockface.

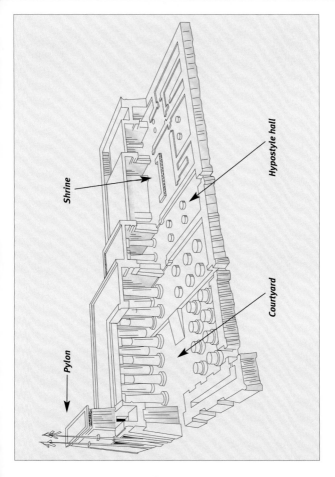

Fig. 3: Section and plan of Karnak temple to Khons.

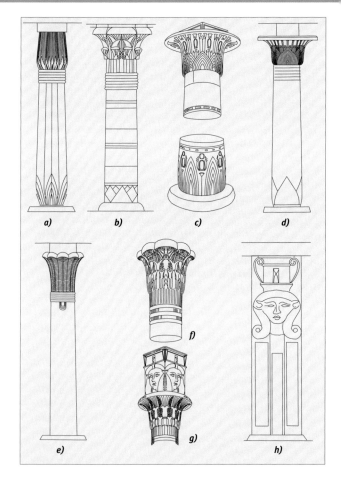

Fig. 4: Columns and Capitals (letters refer to text opposite).

The Temple's Columns and Capitals

One of the most striking elements of Egyptian temple architecture is the massive column crowned by its ornately carved capital. This appears at its most spectacular in the hypostyle hall, a veritable forest of columns, each decorated with carved reliefs glorifying the gods and pharaohs. The largest in Karnak's Temple of Amun measure 21 m (68 ft) high and 3.6 m (nearly 12 ft) in diameter.

Just as the Saqqara sanctuary imitates in stone the wooden structures of domestic building, so the columns express their vegetable origin. The shafts suggest bundles of plant stems, gathered in a little at the base, or emphasized by reed-like forms above the plinth as seen opposite in Fig. 4(a). The bundles of stems are stylized at Queen Hatshepsut's mortuary temple in 16-sided columns, which are precursors of Greek Doric pillars. The capitals emphasize the plant motif in the form of papyrus (b), lotus buds (a), bell-shaped bloom (c and d), palm fronds (e), or a combination of several (f). At Abu Simbel and later at Denderah and Philae, the capitals have the sculpted form of the goddess Hathor's head (g), while at the Hathor Temple in Denderah the goddess's head is incorporated into the design of the columns (h).

Houses of Nobles and Commoners

The ancient Egyptians built for eternity only in their temples and mausoleums. Residential architecture, whether simple houses or aristocratic temples were, apart from stone window frames, doorsteps, lintels and column bases, made of perishable wood and mudbrick.

Thanks to the artisans who fashioned the tombs in the Valley of the Kings, we have an idea of what the houses looked like. They used local materials to build their own homes in stone, some of which have in part survived in the workers' village at Deir El Medinah. They have three or four rooms—living-room, bedroom and storage space, an outdoor kitchen, and a stairway leading to a rooftop area with a low parapet for summertime open-air sleeping.

Nobles' houses as depicted on tomb friezes in the Valley of the Kings had several storeys, with windows high on the walls to restrict the sunlight and hooded vents in the roof to capture and circulate cool breezes.

At Tell El Amarna, Akhenaton's capital, meagre remains of nobles' villas have been excavated to reveal residences of 30 rooms, with toilet and bathroom facilities and an upper storey raised on pillars.

Sculpture, Relief Carvings and Paintings

From the tiny *ushabti* figurines in the tombs acting as servants for the deceased to the colossal statues of Ramses II and his queen proclaiming their superhuman divinity at Abu Simbel, Egyptian sculpture always served a religious or magical purpose. A pharaoh's statue is often shown with a falcon sheltering his head with its outspread wings. This symbolizes the protection of the god Horus. But however stereotyped these poses might be, a certain individuality is also evident, as in an early statue of King Djoser expressing in his severe set of mouth and jaw the determined look of majesty. Sculptures of the oft-portrayed scribe add to his characteristic cross-legged pose a watchful eye or cocked head indicative both of obedience and intelligence.

The common people figure frequently as servants of the royal or noble deceased—cooks, butchers or farmers depicted in polychrome wood or limestone as strikingly as any Flemish peasant of Pieter Brueghel. This realism disappears in the impoverished Middle Kingdom as sculptors confess their inability to carve details of bodies by draping crouching figures in all-concealing cloaks topped by expressionless heads. The prosperous New Kingdom brings about a veritable Renaissance with splendid statues of Queen Hatshepsut, Tuthmosis III, Amenhotep III and their court stewards and architects. Realism is carried to exaggerated length under the revolutionary Akhenaton, but his queen Nefertiti is portrayed with a sensual beauty unmatched in subsequent Egyptian sculpture.

Since mortuary temples and tombs were started under the pharaohs' and nobles' own supervision, the ultimate occupants often died before the decoration was finished. We can thus follow step by step how they were prepared. A grid of vertical and horizontal red lines was drawn on the wall. A first sketch in red was corrected in black and then painted with a powdered tempera pigment mixed with egg-white or other fixative. Scholars have always been astonished by the graphic virtuosity of artists from the every earliest times, notably in the Egyptian Museum's celebrated frieze of Maidum geese dated at 2630 BC. In the specific domain of relief carving, Seti I's temples at Abydos and Karnak and his tomb in Thebes present marvels of dramatic movement and life. Ramses II's battlefield scenes at Karnak and Abu Simbel are too bombastic for some tastes but do give a vivid sense of the great pharaoh's megalomania.

Dynasties	Pharaohs	Date BC	Cultural events
Archaic Period			
1st Dynasty	Narmer	3170	Writing introduced from Mesopotamia
2nd	Unidentified	2800	Gallery tombs at Saqqara
	Khasekhemwy	2700	Tomb sculpture at Abydos
3rd	Djoser	2687–2667	First pyramid at Saqqara
Old Kingdom			
4th	Snoferu	2630–2606	Bent Pyramid, Dahshur Pyramids, mastaba tombs, geese frescoes at Maidum
	Kheops	2606–2583	Great Pyramid, Giza
	Khephren	2575–2550	Sphinx, Giza
5th	Niuserre	2450	Sun Temple, Abu Ghurab
Middle Kingdom		2035–1668	
11th	Mentuhotep II	2010	Beni Hasan rock-cut tombs First temple in Valley of Kings, Thebes
12th	Amenemhet	1991	First obelisks at Heliopolis
	Senusret III	1874–1855	More realistic sculpture
Hyksos		1670–1552	Bronze, silver jewellery
15th			New musical instruments
New Kingdom			
18th	Ahmose I	1552–1524	Royal temple at Abydos
	Amenhotep I	1524–1504	Amun temple, Karnak
	Tuthmosis I	1504–1492	First rock-cut tomb in Valley of Kings
	Hatshepsut	1478–1437	Temple at Deir El Bahri, obelisks at Karnak
	Amenhotep III	1402–1364	Great temple-builder, Luxor Avenue of Sphinxes at Karnak Colossi of Memnon, Thebes
	Akhenaton and Nefertiti	1356–1339	New, sensual sculpture, Tell El Amarna
	Tutankhamun	1339–1329	Tomb treasure
19th	Seti I	1291–1279	Temple to Osiris, Abydos
	Ramses II	1279–1212	Ramesseum, Thebes, Hypostyle hall, Karnak Colossi, Abu Simbel
Last Pharaohs			
21st–30th		1086–332	Cat, baboon, bull shrines
Persians	Darius I	521–486	Temples at Kharga oasis
Ptolemies	Ptolemy I	305–282	Library, Alexandria
	Ptolemy II	286–284	Lighthouse, Alexandria
	Ptolemy III	246–222	Temple of Horus, Edfu
	Last Ptolemies	205–30	Temple of Isis at Philae Double Temple at Kom Ombo Hathor Temple at Denderah

1

2

1. **Sobek:** *Crocodile-headed god.*

2. **Seth:** *Desert god of evil, foreign enemies but also of physical strength.*

3. **Horus:** *Falcon-headed god, symbol of power.*

4. **Hathor:** *Goddess of family and joy, with cow's head, horns or ears.*

5. **Bastet:** *Lioness- or cat-headed goddess of love and war.*

6. **Khnum:** *Ram-headed deity guarding the source of the Nile, creator of human beings.*

7. **Thoth:** *Ibis- or baboon-headed god of writing and scholarship.*

5

Fig. 5: The Egyptian Pantheon.

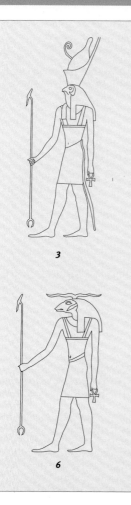

3

6

4

7

Hieroglyphics

The system of writing known as hieroglyphics appeared in Egypt around 3200 BC, when the Sumerians of Mesopotamia were developing their cuneiform script. The ancient Egyptian alphabet dates from around 2700 BC; it combines *phonograms*, signs representing sounds, with *ideograms* expressing meanings. Practically all consonants, hieroglyphs read from right to left, from left to right or, in vertical texts, from top to bottom.

"Hieroglyph" derives from the Greek for "sacred stone-engravings". On leather, wood or papyrus, they sometimes serve as "sketches" to be transferred to stone, the appropriate medium for religious texts intended for eternity. The sacred texts may also appear on these materials in a more cursive form linking these otherwise separate signs in what is known as "hieratic" (religious) script. A shorthand "demotic" (popular) later developed and was used from the 7th century BC for business and literary purposes.

From the last-known sample of hieroglyphs found on the island of Philae near Aswan and dated AD 394 till the invasion of Egypt by Napoleon Bonaparte in 1798, the meaning of Egyptian writing was lost. Lieutenant Pierre Bouchard stationed on the Nile Delta found an ancient engraved slab of black granite in Arab fortifications at Rashid (Rosetta to Europeans). This was the Rosetta Stone later seized by the British and presented to the British Museum. Fortunately for the young French linguist, Jean-François Champollion (1790–1832), a rubbing of the inscription had been made which he was able to decipher in 1822. The inscription proved to be hieroglyphic, demotic and Greek versions of the same text (celebrating the coronation of Ptolemy V in 196 BC). By correlating them with well-known inscriptions like the cartouches of Ramses II and Tuthmosis III, he was able to deduce the dual function of hieroglyphs as sound and meaning.

From his knowledge of the Coptic language, a continuation of ancient Egyptian, Champollion knew that *Ra* means "sun" as in Ramses II, son of the sun-god. He got the *S* sound from the last hieroglyph in *Ptolemaios*, Greek for Ptolemy in the Rosetta inscription. This gave him *Ra-?-s-s*. By comparing the Ramses II and Tuthmosis III cartouches, he located the hieroglyph for the *M*, coming right after the ibis bird sign for the god *Thoth* of whom Tuthmosis was the son—*Mosis*. Proceeding in this way, Champollion compiled a whole hieroglyphic dictionary. Opposite is a chart of sounds for each sign:

a as in hat	f as in full	s as in rings
a as in arm	m as in mull	sh as in shade
i as in tilt	n as in null	k as in king
ee as in reed	r as in rice, but very close to l	k as in basket
y as in yellow	l as in lion	g as in glove
o as in home	h as in hat	t as in cat
oo as in too or w as in wool	strong h as in loch	ch as in church
u as in bull	kh as in Akhbar	d as in dog
b as in bull	ch as in German "ich"	j as in judge
p as in pull	s as in see	

Fig. 6: Approximate pronunciation of the hieroglyphic alphabet.

Royal Cartouches

The simplest form in which you will encounter hieroglyphs is in the cartouches engraved on royal monuments and statues. These shield-like forms inscribe the ruler's principal name or names, the elongated shape symbolizing the universe embraced by the pharaoh. Combining hieroglyphs of sound and meaning, these are some of Egypt's best-known rulers, including Persian, Greek and Roman monarchs who chose to assimilate themselves to pharaohs:

Fig. 7: Royal cartouches.

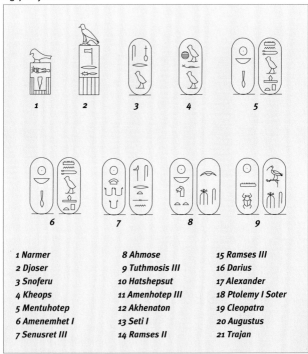

1 Narmer	8 Ahmose	15 Ramses III
2 Djoser	9 Tuthmosis III	16 Darius
3 Snoferu	10 Hatshepsut	17 Alexander
4 Kheops	11 Amenhotep III	18 Ptolemy I Soter
5 Mentuhotep	12 Akhenaton	19 Cleopatra
6 Amenemhet I	13 Seti I	20 Augustus
7 Senusret III	14 Ramses II	21 Trajan

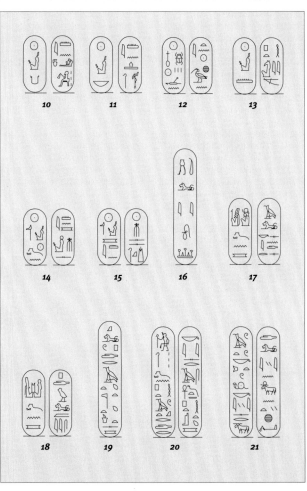

10   11   12   13

14   15   16   17

18   19   20   21

Latest Discoveries

Archaeologists estimate that as much as 90 per cent of all of Egypt's antiquities remain unexcavated. Most spectacular of recent discoveries are underwater remains of Alexandria's gigantic Pharos lighthouse, one of the Seven Wonders of the World that once soared 120 m (393 ft) above the harbour. In addition to hundreds of blocks from the tower's masonry, French divers located in 1995 remains of three colossal statues, a dozen sphinxes and three obelisks. Lying at a depth of 7 m (22 ft), they date either from the Ptolemaic era or back to Ramses II's father, Seti I (1291–1279 BC) and brought here from Heliopolis by the Ptolemies. The first finds have been restored and are displayed in the archaeological gardens of Kom El Dik at Alexandria.

At Luxor, American archaeologists uncovered in 1994 the biggest and most complex of tombs in the Valley of Kings—identified as KV5, containing the combined burial chambers of four sons of Ramses II's 52 offspring. A hypostyle hall leads to a labyrinth with over 110 corridors and chambers burrowing deep into the hillside.

In more recent times, the stone tomb of a noblewoman, Sekhemet Nefret, was excavated near Saqqara in August 2007, and remains of an ancient temple, with well-preserved hieroglyphics and reliefs depicting Ramses II, hidden for centuries behind the walls of a Luxor mosque, have been discovered. Mud walls probably erected to protect the Sphinx from sand were uncovered in 2010, while satellite surveys in 2011 revealed seventeen lost pyramids, and infrared images disclose over 1,000 tombs and 3,000 ancient settlements.

Fig. 8: Pharos of Alexandria, artist's impression.

THE HARD FACTS

To plan your trip, here are some of the practical details you should know about Egypt.

Airports
Most international flights come into Cairo or Alexandria, though some charters also serve El Alamein, Marsa Matruh, Luxor, Hurghada and Sharm El Sheikh. Domestic flights also serve Aswan and Abu Simbel. The terminals provide banking services. Luxor and Cairo airports have facilities for car-hire.

Climate
These days, most hotels, tourist coaches and cruise boats provide good air conditioning, but for outdoors sightseeing choose your season carefully. Though summer is a sizzler—up around 32°C (90°F)—Egypt's predominantly dry heat makes it easier to bear. Cairo is more humid than Luxor and Aswan. The most comfortable time for Europeans to go is in October and November—around 24°C (75°). April and May are also mild, but have some really hot spells. The popular winter holidays from December to February alternate between balmy and cool, averaging 15°C (60°F). The only rain you are likely to run into then is on the Mediterranean coast. And the one place it is always downright cold is before dawn in the desert.

Communications
To get your holiday postcards back home before you do, disguise them as letters inside envelopes, and the Egyptian post office will treat them more seriously. The internet has spread like wildfire. Good hotels have high-speed and often wireless connection, as do some Nile cruisers. Internet cafés abound.

Crime
Egyptians are fundamentally honest. Merchants in the bazaar are not seeking to cheat you, just trying like businessmen anywhere to get the best bargain and keep the customer happy. Pickpockets are much commoner in Europe than in the crowded streets of Egypt. Without undue paranoia, don't tempt the few that do exist anywhere with an open handbag or a wallet in the hip pocket. Leave your valuables in the hotel safe. Lock your luggage

before leaving it with porters at the station or airport.

Driving

Except for short excursions around the Red Sea or Sinai resorts, mostly four-wheel-drive, it is quite simply not recommended to drive yourself in Egypt. In Cairo and other cities, Europeans will find traffic too chaotic, the roads are not always in great condition. Nile Valley highways are not frequently sign-posted enough other than in Arabic. Most car hire firms propose chauffeur-driven rates not much higher than self-drive. If you're still not convinced, remember that driving is (nominally) on the right-hand side, speed limits ignored and traffic lights purely decorative.

Emergencies

Most problems can be handled at your hotel desk. To deal with the special concerns of tourists, Egypt has a Tourist Police, identified as such by a green and white armband and usually speaking some English. They are evident around hotels, at every tourist site and in the city streets, and are always ready to help.

For ambulance service, call the number 123, wherever you are in Egypt.

Your consulate is there only for critical situations, lost pass-ports or worse, but not lost cash or plane tickets.

Essentials

Pack very little. Remember you carry your own bags between hotel, bus and cruise boat. In any case, clothing should be light — cottons are less sticky than synthetics. Add a sweater for cool evenings. Good walking shoes are vital and easy-to-kick-off sandals or moccasins for visiting Muslim homes or mosques. If you need prescribed medicines, take your own, as Egyptian equivalents may be hard to find. Include insect-repellent and a pocket torch (flashlight) — invaluable for the pharaohs' tombs and desert nights.

Formalities

Egypt requires, in addition to a valid passport, a tourist visa for a period of one month. Tour operators usually take care of this as part of the package, but if you are travelling alone, get your visa from the Egyptian consulate before leaving home.

Customs controls are minimal at point of entry, with an official import allowance of 200 cigarettes or 25 cigars or 200 g of tobacco and 1 litre of wine or spirits. The import or export of foreign currency in amounts in excess of the equivalent of US$10,000 must be declared.

The limit for the import of local currency stands at LE5000. The export of Egyptian pounds is forbidden.

Health

No special shots are needed for Egypt at present, but the situation changes, so check with your family doctor before leaving. Get him to prescribe a pill if you are prone to stomach upsets due to change of climate and diet. Make sure your insurance policy covers medical treatment in Egypt. Above all, don't overdo the sun. Take a hat, wear protective creams and, wherever possible, stick to the shade when sightseeing. Dehydration can be a problem, so drink plenty of liquids—make mineral water a habit even when you don't feel thirsty. One other water thought: take your dip in the swimming pool or the sea, not in the Nile, and take mosquito repellent.

Holidays and festivals

Secular holidays are fixed; these are:

January 1	*New Year's Day*
January 7	*Coptic Christmas*
April 25	*Sinai Day*
May 1	*Labour Day*
July 23	*Revolution Day*
October 6	*Armed Forces Day*

Religious holidays wander round the year according to the Muslim lunar calendar. All as moveable as Christian Easter, the most important is the fasting month of Ramadan. The Islamic day starts at sundown, meaning that a religious holiday marked for a particular date in the standard calendar in fact begins on the previous evening.

Languages

English is the most commonly spoken language after Arabic, but you may find French useful as a backup in Cairo or Alexandria. Besides its consecration as the language of diplomacy in negotiating a beach mattress, German is fast becoming a language of commerce in bazaars and restaurants.

Media

Egypt is a good place to forget the affairs of the world, but news-gluttons can get their fill from day-late foreign papers or Egypt's government-run English- (or French-) language dailies. Television in major hotels gets CNN, BBC World Service and French, German and Italian stations by satellite.

Money

The Egyptian pound, abbreviated as LE, is divided into 100 piastres (pt). Coins from 50 piastres to LE1; notes from 5 piastres (rare) to LE200. There are plans to introduce an LE500 note. Bank-notes are printed in Arabic on one side and in English on the other. Coins are rarely given as change.

Money can be exchanged in banks, bureaux de change, and in large hotels and on Nile ships at the official rate. Do not exchange elsewhere. ATMs can be found outside banks in city centres. They deliver clean new notes, but inconveniently large denominations.

Increasingly, shops and restaurants accept credit cards and often prefer them to cash. Travellers cheques are best cashed at the bank or hotel; you will need your passport.

Opening hours

Banks generally open Sunday to Thursday 8.30 a.m. to 2 p.m., though outlets at airports and major hotels are more flexible.

In Cairo, most shops are open 10 a.m. to 7 p.m. in winter and 10 a.m. to 8 p.m. in summer, closing one hour later on Mondays and Thursdays all year round. These times are interrupted for two or three hours for the sacrosanct siesta—official in government shops, closed 2 to 5 p.m. There are no fixed closing hours for shops during the month of Ramadan. Pharmacies stay open late.

Most major museums in Cairo are open every day of the week 9 a.m. to 5.30 p.m., with a Friday break 11.30 a.m. to 1.30 p.m. Smaller museums open only in the morning.

Photography

In many sites and museums it is forbidden to take photographs, as well as in tombs and the entire Valley of the Kings. In Alexandria's National Museum, the Nubian Mueum and the temples of Abydos, Dendera and Edfu, you can take pictures, but without the flash. Photography is also prohibited around airports, bridges and government offices.

Social graces

Contact with ordinary Egyptians is much easier than you might imagine. In the towns, many speak a few words of English, but a handshake and a couple of words of Arabic from you—*min fadlak*, please, or *shokran*, thank you—can work wonders in getting a friendly response.

Remember when you enter a mosque, besides taking off your shoes, modest dress is essential —no shorts or bare shoulders. Keep your swimwear for the beach or swimming pool.

Tipping

The Middle Eastern institution of *baksheesh* is not the casual corruption imagined by some sceptical foreign visitors; it's an accepted acknowledgement of services rendered. Tour-group leaders usually take care of local guides at monuments or museums, but beyond the customary personal tip for waiters, hotel staff or taxi drivers, have a supply of 1- or 5-pound notes ready when you're out on your own, for helpful caretakers at mosques and ancient temples or beach attendants looking after your mattress. LE5 is about equivalent to 53p, 0.63 euros or 82 US cents.

Toilets

Men have it easier than women, but in the absence of good public facilities, everybody's safest bet is a respectable-looking hotel or restaurant. Give a small tip to the lady supplying toilet paper; she has to buy it in the first place.

Tourist Information Offices

Egypt's Tourist Information Offices provide maps, brochures and up-to-date information on opening hours. They can even help you with a personal guide for some place not covered in your itinerary. They have counters at the airports and main railway stations as well as in all the major towns.

Transport

If time is no object, take to the river. A luxury Nile cruise is a wonderful experience, but failing that, do take the more modest water-bus in Cairo or a felucca at Luxor or Aswan.

Fly inside Egypt for really long distances, but from Aswan to Abu Simbel, for instance, a dawn coach ride can be a wonderful way of discovering the desert. Trains from Cairo go up the Nile Valley to Luxor and Aswan or across to Alexandria.

In the capital, take a taxi, as the bus is just too hectic, with people hanging on to the exterior, though the less crowded underground can be an exhilarating adventure. Do not be surprised if you are sometimes expected to share your taxi with a stranger. Major hotels operate limousine services, not too expensive if there are plenty of you: agree on the price before setting off.

In smaller towns, you can ride in a horse-drawn *calèche*, but be sure to agree on a price, the drivers tend to hassle, and may insist on taking you where *they* want instead of where you want (especially in Luxor). Sightseeing at Luxor or Aswan can be more fun with a rented bicycle. And why not let a camel or donkey take you to the pyramids or around the royal tombs in the Valley of the Kings?

Voltage

Count on 220-volt, 50-cycle AC with European-style sockets for two round pins.

SAY IT

ENGLISH	EGYPTIAN ARABIC	NUMBERS	
Standard greetings	Salaam alekum (Peace be with you)	1	wahad
standard reply	Alekum salaam (with you, peace)	2	itnayn
		3	talata
Good morning	Sbah el kheer	4	arba'a
Good evening	Missa el kheer	5	khamsa
Goodbye	Maas salaam	6	sitta
Now	El an	7	saba'a
Today	El yoom	8	tamanya
Yesterday	Ems	9	tisa'a
Tomorrow	Ghodwa	10	ashara
Later	Minbad	11	hidashar
Yes	Naam	12	itnashar
No	La	13	talattashar
Please	Min fadlak	14	arba'atashar
Thank you	Shokran	15	khamastashar
You're welcome	Afon	16	sittashar
How much?	Bikam?	17	saba'tashar
Too much	Yessir	18	tamantashar
Go away! (to children)	Imshi!	19	tisa'tashar
Enough/stop	Bass!	20	ishrin

Port Said

200 m

N

Outer
Harbour

Shipyard
Harbour

Alaresh Way

PORT FUAD

Suez
Canal

Ferry

Commercial
Harbour

Suez Canal
Authority

El Zaeem Ghandi

Al Salam
Mosque

Military
Museum

M

Casino
Palace

Shokre Alikotie

Elsmailia - Port Said

Tarth Albahr 8

National
Museum

Saad Zaghloul

Araf

Sadke Basha

Algomhoria

Mahmoud

Safia Zaghlol

Roman
Catholic
Cathedral

Abd Alsalam

Ahmed Orabe

Said - Port

Abbas

Ghrab - Port Said

Al Rahma
Mosque

Shari el-Nahda

Kanater

El

Alhabashe

Algomhoria

Araf

El Zaeem Ghandi

Araf

Governorate

Ahmed

Abd Alsalam

Orabe

Said

Safia Zaghlol

Al Abbasi
Mosque

Port - Said

El Ismailia - Port Said

Ahmed Mahar

El Ismailia

Shar el-Nahda

Mostafa Kamel

Alasawe

Alghaze Khalat

Alsheret Ali

(Alshohada)
Mohamed Ali Sabkan

Ahmed Ibrahim
Almahde

El Zaeem Ghandi

Alkomash Alkadem Tarth Albahr

Alex - Port Said

Abd Alsalam

Ahmed

Abbas

Askandaria

Ismailia

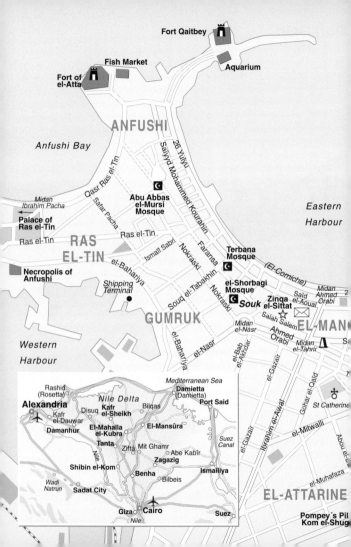

Fort Qaitbey

Fish Market

Aquarium

Fort of
el-Atta

ANFUSHI

Anfushi Bay

Qasr Ras el-Tin

26 Yulyu

Saiyid Mohammed Kourahin

*Midan
Ibrahim Pacha*

Safar Pacha

Abu Abbas
el-Mursi
Mosque

**Palace of
Ras el-Tin**

Ras el-Tin

**RAS
EL-TIN**

Ras el-Tin

Ismail Sabri

Faransa

Nokraski

Terbana
Mosque

*Eastern
Harbour*

(El-Corniche)

**Necropolis of
Anfushi**

el-Bahariya

el-Shorbagi
Mosque

Souq el-Tabakhin

Nokraski

Said
el-Aouai

*Midan
Ahmed
Orabi*

2

*Shipping
Terminal*

Zinqa
el-Sittat

Souk

GUMRUK

Midan
el-Nasr

Salah Salem

EL-MAN

el-Bahariya

el-Nasr

Ahmed
Orabi

Midan
el-Tahrir

el-Gazair

el-Bab
el-Akhdar

*Western
Harbour*

el-Gazair

Ibrahim el-Awal

St Catherine

el-Mitwalli

EL-ATTARINE

Mediterranean Sea

Rashid
(Rosetta)

Nile Delta

Damietta
(Damietta)

Port Said

Alexandria

Disuq

Kafr
el-Sheikh

Bilqas

Kafr
el-Dauwar

El-Mahalla
el-Kubra

El-Mansûra

Gohar el-Qaid

Damanhur

Tanta

Zifta

Mit Ghamr

Abe Kabîr

*Suez
Canal*

el-Muhafaza

Shibin el-Kom

Zagazig

Benha

Bilbeis

Ismailiya

Abou el-

*Wadi
Natrun*

Sadat City

Giza

Cairo

Suez

Nile

**Pompey's Pil
Kom el-Shug**

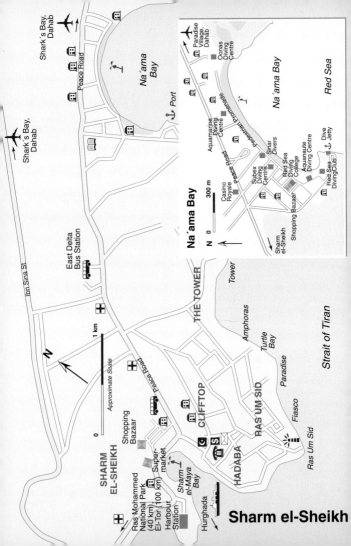

Sharm el-Sheikh

Shark's Bay, Dahab

Shark's Bay, Dahab

Peace Road

Na´ama Bay

Port

Ibn Sina St

East Delta Bus Station

Ras Mohammed National Park (40 km) El-Tor (100 km)

SHARM EL-SHEIKH

Shopping Bazaar

Super-market

Sharm el-Maya Bay

Harbour Station

Hurghada

Peace Road

THE TOWER

Tower

CLIFFTOP

HADABA

RAS UM SID

Amphoras

Turtle Bay

Paradise

Fiasco

Ras Um Sid

Strait of Tiran

0   1 km

Approximate Scale

Na´ama Bay

Paradise Village, Dahab

Oonas Diving Centre

Na´ama Bay

Red Sea

Aquamarine Diving Centre

Pedestrian Promenade

Peace Road

Sinai Divers

Subex Diving Centre

Red Sea Diving College

Aquanaute Diving Centre

Dive Jetty

Red Sea Diving Club

Casino Royale

Shopping Bazaar

Sharm el-Sheikh

N   0   300 m

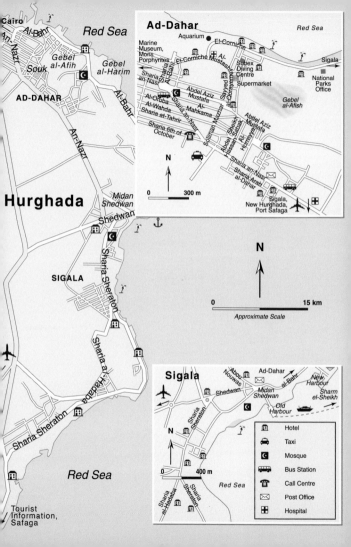

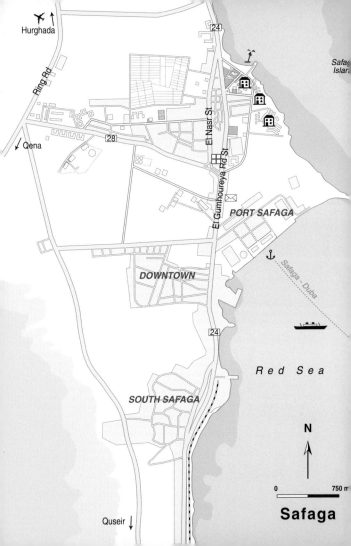

Safaga

General editor
Barbara Ender-Jones

Design
Karin Palazzolo

Layout
Luc Malherbe

Photo credits
Bernard Joliat: p. 1
Mickael David: p. 2
(Tutankhamun, Horus falcon)
François Ender: p. 2 (fish)
istockphoto.com/Podgoresk:
p.2 (Bedouin)

Maps
Elsner & Schichor;
JPM Publications,
Mathieu Germay

Copyright © 2012, 1994
JPM Publications S.A.
12, avenue William-Fraisse,
1006 Lausanne, Switzerland
information@jpmguides.com
http://www.jpmguides.com/

Printed in Switzerland
13688.00.11174
Edition 2012